Praise For

WINNING THE GAME OF LIFE

"Chantell has always been an amazing sister and an inspiration to me as her younger brother. Like my father, Chantell has incredible drive and determination. I will never forget watching her basketball games from the bleachers and being so proud. She always gave it her all. During the years I struggled in school Chantell was there to help me. And even now, no matter how busy she seems to be, Chantell finds time to mentor and pour into the lives of others. Through this book, Chantell shares her story and life lessons that inspire and encourage. I am very blessed to have Chantell as my sister, and I always value her wisdom and our time together."

Robert Mayes, MBA
CEO of Columbia Southern Education Group
President, Columbia Southern University

"Chantell's story is one of perseverance, persistence, faith, and, yes, winning. What is truly remarkable is not how Chantell won, but how she redefines winning. For Chantell, winning is not about her personal victories, but about how she can pay back those who mentored her and pay forward anyone who is willing to learn along with her the lessons of her life. Her story is not just inspirational; it's relational. This book won't make life's challenges go away, but you will have a new mentor to help you through those challenges."

Bob Alsop
President of Waldorf U'
Forest City, Iov

"Winning the Game of Life by Chantell Cooley is a book that offers life insights, lessons and reminders for readers of all ages. With heart, humor and real-life experiences, Chantell lays out the truths that can help us all power through life's challenges and play to win! Chantell's reflections on her own family's struggles and successes form a simple and thoughtful outline for making the most of the lives God has given us. This book is not only a powerful tool for personal growth it's also an ideal study-guide for small groups!"

Eric McHaney
Chief Marketing Officer
Columbia Southern Education Group

"This is a fabulous story of insightful perseverance about Chantell and her family's journey. Read it twice; once for the story and again to contemplate the 'Lessons,' including the impact the lessons learned in athletic competition during the formative years can have throughout life."

Randy P. Juhl, Ph.D.
Dean Emeritus and
Distinguished Service Professor Emeritus of Pharmacy
University of Pittsburgh

"Winning the Game of Life offers a dynamic and exciting reading experience. Chantell's story resonates with all of us at some level and for me at a deeply personal level. I think many of us had challenging upbringings for one reason or another. And regardless of how fortunate someone's circumstances may seem from a distance, there is always a story behind the story. To that point, I think there are lessons behind the lessons. Take time to reflect on the story and the 100+ lessons. You would enjoy this book in a group setting too, as you discuss the lessons through the lenses of the experiences and impressions of others. If there is one more lesson I would add, it is this: 'Always look for another mountain to climb!' Beyond personal success, this book is a challenge to go the next level and I accept."

Bobby Halton
Editor-in-Chief, Fire Engineering Magazine
Education Director, FDIC International
Magazine Editorial Director, Fire Rescue and
Fire Apparatus and Emergency Equipment

"Chantell (AKA Champion) and her family are absolutely amazing in their perseverance and resilience. Winning the Game of Life is an inspiring book about their journey in life, its challenges and opportunities. It is a wonderful example of facing and overcoming difficulties. You will find imbedded in the book profound lessons and rules of life beneficial to everyone. I like!"

Gery C. Hochanadel, Ph.D.
Vice President of Academic Affairs
Cleveland University-Kansas City

"I have had the great fortune of knowing and mentoring Chantell Mayes Cooley since she was 19 years old! Chantell is a unique and gifted speaker on several fronts with enormous passion, sincerity and great wit. It has been one of the joys of my life to participate in her journey and witness her advance and successes along the way.

Chantell is a woman of faith and wears it well. She knows what it is to look beyond with hope for what cannot be seen with the natural eye and be moved to that place that seemed so far from reality. As you read her book, Winning the Game of Life, you will know and sense that she is not just telling a story or espousing certain principles. She shares some of herself with you, the reader. I am so proud of her intense drive to inspire others to make a difference in their lives, as she has been able to do herself."

Buford Lipscomb
Chairman of the Board of Trustees, Waldorf University &
Senior Pastor | President
Liberty Church | Liberty Network International

"What a refreshing look at the making of a champion. Chantell Cooley beautifully illustrates how to grow, persist and work hard to fulfill your dreams. You will be encouraged and challenged through these practical tips on how to become a champion, influence others, change your world and create lasting legacy."

Elizabeth Tiam-Fook
Founder of The Elisha Company International
Maricopa, Arizona

"As one of Chantell's teammates, I can say there was never a dull moment. Every team needs a spark, someone who plays with such intensity that others can't help but feed off of it, and for us that person was Chantell. She showed up to every game ready to win and expected nothing less. I've always appreciated Chantell's feisty, no-quit attitude which has now translated into a lifestyle of winning and success. This book will change your life."

Melissa Wilson
Pastor
Liberty Church, Foley, AL

"When I was younger, I had the opportunity of playing high school basketball with Chantell. As I reminisce over those games, she was usually going so hard and fast defensively that she would slide into metal chairs or be propelled into the bleachers, but she always managed to quickly get back up and go another round. When I think back to Chantell and her family, going through the many struggles of life, it's like watching Romans 5:3 in action: 'Not only so, but we also glory in our sufferings, because we know that suffering produces perseverance; perseverance, character; and character, hope.' For Chantell, hope's foundation has been a difficult build. The solid framework of her character is definitely 'His' blood, mixed with her humble sweat and tears. Yet, the common denominator is perseverance. Chantell's pursuit of the Kingdom of God is contagious and encouraging."

Melinda Adams Bachtold
Former High School Basketball Teammate
Elberta, AL

"There are two kinds of truth in the world. Truth and Qualified Truth. Qualified Truth always trumps Truth because it comes only from a life that has lived it out and proven its validity. I've known Chantell for many years, and the nuggets in this book have come from the testings and fires of Qualified Truth. Enjoy."

JP Wilson
Lead Pastor
Liberty Church, Foley, AL

"I have known Chantell and her family long enough to recognize and understand the heart-felt feelings they have for others. The thoughts and suggestions in Chantell's book are timely, especially for those early in their career and also when life seems to treat you unfairly. I wish I had had these types of influences early in my 40-year career in the fire service; I might not have struggled so desperately."

Forney Howard
Retired Fire Chief

"This is a great book, a moving account of a difficult passage, full of heart and wisdom. It is an offering from a true spiritual friend, boss and mentor. Now I know where her passion and commitment to change lives started, and I have been blessed to see her and her company grow. The ones who are crazy enough to think they can change the world are the ones who do."

Rick Cooper,
BS (USN Retired)
Vice President of Business Development and Military Initiatives
Columbia Southern Education Group, Inc.

"It is truly an honor to call Chantell Cooley my friend. After reading this book and understanding her journey, it only validates what I already know about her. Chantell has learned from her own life, and is filled with true wisdom and insight. Winning the Game of Life presents lessons that will equip you with true, time-tested wisdom. This book will change how you view your life, and if you dare to apply the lessons, you can actually change your life for the better."

Melanie Martin
Owner of Melanies, Inc & MTwo Interiors
Orange Beach, AL

"Winning the Game of life is an amazing read! Chantell has woven the secrets to success, utilizing the peaks and valleys from her personal life, her family life and fundamentals from one of the most exciting games we know. The life lessons embedded throughout the book will inspire you to succeed and encourage you to never give up. This is definitely a book you'll want in your inspirational toolbox."

Lee West
Executive Pastor
Liberty Church
One Church. Multiple Locations.

"Powerful, practical, proven lessons in winning the game of life . . . an awesome story of lessons learned. Chantell Cooley shares her powerful life story of faith, family and hard work to reach life goals which are uplifting, yet she goes a step further. This book provides insight and lessons that the reader can put to practical application in their own career and private lives."

Rodney O. Anderson,
MG US Army (Ret)
President LDR Consulting, LLC

"Winning the Game of Life will inspire you to keep hope alive in the midst of life's challenges. Chantell Cooley demonstrates the importance of believing things will get better and to never give up as she shares from her own life experiences. She uses practical advice that will encourage you to go beyond what you have imagined for your life and achieve more than you ever thought you could. How do you keep hope alive in the midst of difficulties and challenges? This book will remind you of the value of prayer and faith, of laughter, of family, and perseverance during those difficult times."

Sue S. Butts
Vice President, SPHR, SHRM-SCP
Columbia Southern Education Group, Inc.

"Winning the Game of Life is a peek into the inspirational lives of the Mayes family. I've known this family for many years, and they are the most upbeat, positive, generous people I know. I also know that they pray about everything and it is not surprising to learn that in her early years, Chantell and her parents relied heavily on prayer. They depended on the Lord when they were in need, gave thanks to the Lord when they had an abundance and celebrated together each small success. This book is full of valuable lessons to be practiced and applied throughout life."

Dawn Cranston
Head of School
South Baldwin Christian Academy
Gulf Shores, AL

"Chantell Cooley's book Winning the Game of Life is a story of passion and determination to go after it. It is inspiring, and will grab you to move yourself forward in life. Chantell is capable of mentoring and helping others because she has allowed herself to be mentored. She is the real deal and gives real-life experiences and lessons that will change your life."

John Thompson
Deputy Executive Director and COO
National Sheriffs' Association
Washington D.C. Metro Area

"Chantell Cooley's book Winning the Game of Life is a heartwarming story about the character of a young girl applying the lessons learned in her youth, and how those life lessons can be a road map to success for those willing to adhere to those principles."

Dick Corcoran, JD, CFP®
Wealth Management
Executive Vice President
The First National Bank in Sioux Falls, SD

"Where else can you learn over 100 powerful life lessons wrapped around a compelling, amazing, heart-touching personal story? Embracing and integrating any one of these lessons can radically transform your life. Thank you, Chantell, for your transparency, sharing your struggles, and most importantly, for clearing a path so we can all be winners at the Game of Life."

Dr. Jim Harris
Author, Speaker & Executive Advisor
Author of 14 award-winning books including, "Our Unfair Advantage: Unleash the Power of the Holy Spirit in Your Business"

"We have all met people that create a strong first impression, and you know immediately that they are something special. That was my first take on Chantell. The passion, commitment and her love of education was right there on the surface. What is most important to me is that her priority is not to further her own self interest but rather to channel all efforts into serving her students with the aim to make their lives better. She is an educationist and also a wife, mother, business woman and minister. And Chantell, through her relentless energy, passion and great ideas, forges all of that together in everything she does. In Winning the Game of Life, you will encounter this amazing woman and also be a recipient and beneficiary of her talents and passion. I am very grateful to be her friend."

David L. Weber, Sr, M.D.
Director, Waldorf University Board
Waldorf University Distinguished Alumnus
CEO and Chairman of the Board, retired, Wenatchee Valley Medical Center/
Confluence Health, Wenatchee, Washington

"I love Winning the Game of Life because it shows the importance of giving 100% and never giving up, no matter the circumstances. I've known Chantell Cooley for quite awhile. Her potential is enormous, but she also has that rare ability to see the potential in others. If you doubt your potential, then read this book to find encouragement. Winning the Game of Life is nothing short of transformational. It will help you transform into the champion you already are on the inside. Pass it on."

Dr. Marilyn Hickey
President and Founder
Marilyn Hickey Ministries

EDITORS' NOTES

"Chantell's story is rich with emotion. It is packed with practical life, career and business lessons from the world of sports that will empower the reader to succeed at the game of life. In this book you will discover how important the 'little' things are to your success. You will learn the value of family and teams; how to build a solid foundation for your desired future; how to deal with the down-times when life seems at a standstill; and how to live in the moment, ready for that opportunity of a lifetime."

Michelle Ofori-Ansah
Founder
PrimeDoor Media and Marketing
Dallas, TX
www.PrimeDoor.org

"There is the rich dad and there is the poor dad, and then there are the likes of Chantell and her mother, Mimi: women of substance and fortitude, wise, strong and caring, who stand by you, encourage and counsel you through thick and thin. As an entrepreneur starting my own business, I can identify with their story and struggles as they have been those of me and my wife. If I had read a book like this earlier in life, I would have made fewer mistakes in my personal life and career, and would have avoided a lot of pain and heartache. The lessons Chantell gives are born from real life experience, and they will challenge and equip you for your own journey. This book is for every young man and woman, and indeed, everyone seeking to excel and succeed in life. Keep it close and read it often."

Solomon Ofori-Ansah
Founder and President
Isosports International, Inc
Dallas, TX
www.IsoSoccer.com

WINNING
THE GAME
OF LIFE

CHANTELL M. COOLEY

Published by:
Cooley Communications
21982 University Lane
Orange Beach, AL 36561

ISBN #978-0-9976907-1-2 (paperback)
ISBN #978-0-9776907-2-9 (eBook)

Cover Design: Renato Vieira

THE STORY BEHIND THE COVER DESIGN

There is a man climbing a mountain, out of a dark valley, but you see a second mountain, at a higher level, beyond him in a much brighter place. That represents the next phase. Once you conquer one mountain or overcome a difficulty, you will invariably have to climb another and conquer the next challenge. But this time it will be from a higher and better vantage point.

The man climbing the mountain is carrying a bag. That symbolizes his legacy, plans and purpose in life. As we travel through life, there are things that have been passed down to us that must be cherished. We must carry them with us as we continue to seek our purpose and meaning in life.

It is as though the man is walking through a chess piece. This is because the game of life is strategic and mental like the game of chess, and to win it one has to be very deliberate and purposeful.

The chess piece is the Queen, and that is because the queen is the only piece that can move in any direction and any number of spaces. That symbolizes the freedom and liberty we have as humans. We are not bound to failure or to a certain status in life. We have options, but we must make the choice. As free moral agents, we have the liberty and power to choose.

Finally, the title: *Winning The Game Of Life* is written with "Winning" the lightest and the rest in bold. This is because while winning is important, the most essential thing, the focus, is how we live our lives. The emphasis of this book, more than anything, is on Life.

Renato Vieira
Graphic Designer
Dallas, TX

DEDICATION

I wanted to take this time to write about the people who are a part of my family legacy, and show my appreciation for their encouragement, love and support. It is important to understand how God will use people in your life to carry your legacy further. It is our duty to step up to the plate and pursue our purpose. When we do, our legacy is strengthened and taken to the next level. My children will carry my legacy even further than I have. As they step into it, God will open new doors of opportunities, but it will always point back to the legacy.

I am happy to dedicate my book to the following:

Tommy Cooley: To my husband who has been there for me and always supported my dreams and aspirations. He has helped me make this book a reality. Thank you for helping me to continue to dream big.

Dylan Cooley: To my son who I am so proud of. Watching your chapter of high school close and expecting a new chapter to begin in college, I have no doubt you will take my legacy to new levels. Thank you for always being proud of me in front of your friends. I love you. God has given you talent and a vision for big things in your life. GO after those, and hit the mark!

Brooke Cooley: To my beautiful daughter who has that entrepreneur spirit, and is the most talented and creative person I know. Thank you for believing in my vision for writing books. You have always been there for me. Go after your dreams! You can do it!

Mimi Mayes: To my mom, who has always encouraged me to believe in myself. You were always my example for how to follow after God with all your heart. Thank you for giving back and always praying for me every day.

Solomon and Michelle Ofori-Ansah: I would like to thank my editors, who believed in me enough to take on this project. Thank you for listening to me and for understanding my story. You are a part of my legacy now by helping me to write this book. You are two special people with an amazing talent for writing.

TABLE OF CONTENTS

ACKNOWLEDGMENTS

I am where I am today because of the help of many. Some made huge sacrifices, and others were just there to wipe a tear. But together their lives, love, encouragement and support helped shaped me for success. I am very grateful to them, and glad that I am able to show my appreciation in a special way.

"Just go for it." One word from my mom and I was up and ready to give basketball a shot. Both of my parents coached me and prepared me for my first tryouts, even though their skills were rusty from not playing the game since their youth. And after I won a place on the team, my parents were always there to lift me up when things got tough, teaching me to never quit. Because of them, I had the privilege very distinguished few have had, of playing on a team that made it all the way to state and won the championship. I was coached by the best, played with the best, and I learned some of the greatest lessons that have made me who I am today. I will always be grateful to my parents, Robert and Mimi Mayes.

I want to give a special thanks to my brother and boss, Robert Jr. You have always been with me through all the hard times. Growing up, your presence in my life was comforting and inspiring. It challenged me and brought the big girl out of me, and is very much appreciated even now. Thanks for believing in your big sister and always pushing me to go beyond what I thought I could do in life and in business. I believe in you too. The whole world is your playground, and I can't wait to see all that you will accomplish in the future.

Since my late teens, Pastor Buford and Ann Lipscomb have mentored me, speaking into my life and steering me into my destiny. They hold a special place in my heart. Pastor JP and

Melissa Wilson got me on the right path to serve God with all my heart, and they continue to push me to reach for more of Him, even today. I can never thank them enough. Marilyn Hickey is a friend and mentor. She inspires me and is always willing to lend her voice to push me toward my goals. I will always be grateful for her kindness.

I want to also acknowledge my sophomore and junior year high school coach, Harry Breland. He was brilliant in how he explained plays, and always had a way to motivate you to do more than you thought you could do. Beyond the game, he also coached us to be better in life. I was lucky to have someone like him in my life, especially during those impressionable years. Thank you for teaching me the basics of the game, developing confidence in me and laying the foundation for me to be a champion in life.

Wayne Folkes, my senior year high school basketball coach, deserves special mention too. He was great for me and my team. He was the type of coach you would want to do everything you could to please. He knew how to challenge you to reach deeper, to play harder, smarter and never to be intimidated. I know I have had great success in the corporate world because of his influence and leadership in my life. Thank you Coach Folkes, for believing in me, seeing my talents above all else and using me in spite of my many flaws. I am sure you rolled your eyes about all those times I missed free throws, but you always smiled and said, "You will get it next time." Because you cared, it made me care, and I learned to play hard for my team.

And finally, I would like to say a big thank you to Solomon and Michelle Ofori-Ansah who believed in my dream to write books. Their patience and support have given me such strength and more determination to write. They have taken my writing to another level.

FOREWORD

What can really happen in our lives if we dare to believe? What if, in spite of your current situation, you begin to believe that things could become different and can actually change for the better? Is it possible that you could rise above those circumstances? I am convinced that you will. Everyone who has dared to believe has experienced change.

However, believing is one thing, and perseverance is another. The power in Chantell's story is that she and her family do more than believe; they persevere. They fight. The darker it got, the stronger their faith and resolve became.

I am also amazed at how Chantell and her family stood together and made sacrifices as a family. That is a challenge to all of us and our families. In our darkest hours, wouldn't it be nice to turn to either side and see your family empathizing, comforting and cheering you on? How about friends who bring timely help when all seems lost? Where does one get such friends, such loyalty? This book will teach you how to succeed at the social game. It emphasizes the importance of building strong and lasting relationships, presenting vivid evidence of the impact those relationships have on your life and success.

I love *Winning the Game of Life* because it shows the importance of giving 100% and never giving up, no matter the circumstances. I've known Chantell Cooley for quite awhile. Her potential is enormous, but she also has that rare ability to see the potential in others.

If you doubt your potential, then read this book to find encouragement. *Winning the Game of Life* is nothing short of transformational. It will help you transform into the champion you already are on the inside. Pass it on.

-Dr. Marilyn Hickey
President and Founder
Marilyn Hickey Ministries

TESTIMONIAL

For 37 years I have coached baseball, and for 32 of those years I coached basketball as well. In my long career I have had the opportunity to coach many students in different places and at different times. Over time the memory of even the best and most cherished of them becomes dim and eventually fades. But there are a few names and faces that defy the test of time because of who they are and what they symbolize. One of these is Chantell Mayes. Even 30 years after meeting and coaching her at Oak Grove High School, the name Mayes still rings a bell and brings back heartfelt memories.

I remember Chantell as a player that made everybody on the team better, including the coach. She had many talents as a player; however, her greatest contribution and most admirable ability was her tenacious defense. She was relentless in her pursuit of the basketball, and it often paid off with her stealing the ball.

All our reserve players had a vital role in our successful run in the playoffs. Led by Chantell's hustle and physical style of play, they provided us with competitive practices that made us Champions. Chantell and the rest were just what the doctor ordered. You could tell that she took pride in competing at a high level.

Chantell was a team player who cared about her team, and she demonstrated it by giving her all in practices and in each game. I was blessed to have been her coach. She reinforces what we coaches try to teach daily—that you gain life lessons from your experiences in sports.

I believe that because of Chantell's willpower, her faith and her quest for success God has rewarded her.

-Harry Breland
Head Basketball Coach
Oak Grove High School, Hattiesburg, MS

TESTIMONIAL

I remember my first year as head coach for Oak Grove High School. I was excited about my team, but I had concerns about team leadership as some experienced seniors were not returning that year. However, in our first game against Perry Central High School, a very talented team, it became very apparent that my concerns were unfounded.

The score did not end as I had hoped, but I discovered "Mayes!" Chantell brought her game, and played with a passion that set the tone for the year. She was always focused, motivated and had a never-quit attitude that inspired all her teammates to play at a higher level. There was no slacking or not-giving-your-best when Chantell was around. She walked the walk with her positive attitude, faith and her love for her teammates and school. As a leader, she conducted herself on and off the court admirably, and helped develop future leaders for my teams for years to come.

Truly, I thought I was supposed to teach these young ladies basketball, and a little about life, but I learned a lot from Chantell. We did have success over the next several years going to the playoffs, winning records and having some of our girls playing at the next level. Chantell was a young lady who helped lay that strong foundation for a winning attitude and tradition for the game of basketball at Oak Grove High School, but more importantly for the game of life.

Our mascot for Oak Grove High School is the Warriors. Webster's dictionary defines a *warrior* as a person who fights in battles, and is known for having courage and skill. Chantell exemplifies these qualities as a person, a woman of faith and a leader. As a Coach, I could never be prouder. She will forever be a big-time Warrior in my book.

-Wayne Folkes
Assistant Superintendant of Education
Lamar County School District

INTRODUCTION

In this book, I tell you the story of my family, our struggles, and the difficulties that we almost did not overcome. We were a family, not divided but stuck together in purpose. You will see how we fought to discover and keep our legacy alive, and founded Columbia Southern University, one of the largest online institutions in America. In addition, I take you on an adventure, to my days as "Mayes" on a high school basketball team in Mississippi, where a Champion was born. I give an in-depth look into the challenges I faced, how I overcame, the lessons I learned and how those experiences impacted me, and still do to this day.

We are all at different stages of life and in our pursuit of success. Perhaps you have positive movement at the moment. You are going forward and things are clicking along, or perhaps it is the other way round. You are sliding backwards and just can't seem to gain ground to stop. Or maybe you are moving sideways, going round and round in circles and just can't figure out how to break into the next level. There are some who are going through those hard times in very dry places and feeling all alone. They can't even tell where they are in life right now, because everything is so out of control and nothing is working out. They are just quite frankly stuck in a rut. They have been in this place before, and can't get out of the same familiar place.

Whatever your story is, I hope you can relate to mine and find encouragement, because I have been there in one form or another. As you read through this chapter of my life, I want to encourage you to relate to my circumstances. But most importantly, I want to challenge you to take a second look at your life. First of all, examine where you are in life, and dare to ask the hard questions. Are you making the most out of your circumstances? Because as dissatisfied as you may be with where you are, there is still some good there. Though it may not look promising right now, it still holds the key to that next level, that wonderful place that you are dreaming about.

My purpose in writing is to encourage you to have hope in whatever situation you find yourself, and to never give up on the possibilities that life holds. If you have already given up on your dreams, you can revive and begin to pursue them again. This book will inspire and empower you with practical, day-to-day lessons that will make your journey to success a little easier and hopefully, a little shorter. My family and I struggled for years before success came to us, but that doesn't have to be your story. It doesn't matter what your position in life is or what you have been through, you too can become a success. The hard days will come, but facing them and pushing through is the key to unlocking your future. One of the things I say daily is, "Keep moving forward!"

Chapter 1

A CINDERELLA STORY

We don't fully understand the experiences of our childhoods while we are still living them. It's only in retrospect, as grownups, that we are able to appreciate their intricacies and how they fuel our life purpose. During your childhood, I think passions are developed. It all depends on what you went through and how hard you had it. Everything we go through in our formative years will later translate into our purpose or have some impact on it. If you were raised needing financial stability, then as you get older you will have passion in those areas. You may be surprised to realize that if you are looking for your purpose in life, you just have to take a trip down memory lane to find it.

MY STORY, YOUR HOPE

When I was a child, I thought my life was great. It wasn't until I looked back, as an adult, that I realized all the obstacles my family faced and the struggles that we almost didn't overcome. Growing up, my parents, Robert and Mimi Mayes, and my younger brother, Robert Jr., and I lived in East Texas. There was nothing about me or my family that resembled anything remotely close to greatness or wealth. We were your average typical family trying to survive, and we had very little money left over to afford vacations or other luxuries.

My parents were high achievers. They dreamed of being able to be financially stable, to pay our bills and be debt free. It started out just wanting to have enough groceries, a house and a car, a simple life. That wasn't asking for much, but it was hard to get even that to work out. As a family we struggled from the time I was in third grade. From that point on, my childhood was a string of unfamiliar towns, new people and homes that were constantly being foreclosed upon. Leaving those homes was the hardest part of my childhood.

There were times we seemed to have had a lot, but most times we had very little. There were days I am not even sure how we ended up with food on the table. But somehow God brought us through with a smile on our faces. Yes, we didn't have much, but we did have each other. We were a very close family which I believe made all the difference in the world. We always found time that we could enjoy spending with each other. And while we felt lack, I never felt *less than*, because my family loved and supported each other in the midst of it all.

Some of my happiest memories can also be traced back to those hard days. I can remember us throwing our own party. It was just the four of us, but why not? We had some chips and dip and told funny stories. I think that did help us carry on even when everything looked bleak and hopeless. I remember a family vacation in Florida; my Dad had worked hard and saved all year long just to be able to scrape the money together for it. We talked about it and dreamed of the day when we could pack up and start our trip to Florida. For Robert and I, that is still one of our best memories from childhood.

MOM'S TEARS

My father was a visionary and an entrepreneur with a very strong talent in sales. He would see opportunity under every rock and dreamed of being successful in life. He was a man of conviction, and so he would work very hard on his dreams. However, his journey into success was a long and painful one. My father failed many times as he tried to climb the ladder of success. My mom, who was the rock behind him, was always there for him. She pushed him to keep going for his dreams and to never give up.

The frequent hard times Dad went through meant that our homes were foreclosed upon a lot. Many times, as we moved out, we would leave behind all of our personal belongings. The only things we could take were the things that fit into the truck or trailer we were leaving town with. We could never afford more than one trip. As a child, I can remember crying because I had to leave behind most of my toys and books during one of our moves. I have a vivid memory of my mom having to look away as she walked out of one house, leaving many of her cherished childhood possessions. One time we had to leave so much behind, we called a friend and asked him to sell our belongings and send us the money to set up our next home.

Our life as a family was very erratic. At one point, we moved seven times in the span of two years. We lived wherever we could, by whatever means we had. If the air conditioner in the car went out or the element in the dryer broke down, it would be months before we would have enough money to get either fixed. So we would roll the windows down and suffer the heat, or hang our clothes up all over the house to dry. Looking back, I don't know how we made it. We came so close to living on the streets, but fortunately it never reached that point. We were always able to scrape together enough to start again.

FIGHTING YOUNG

For Robert Jr. and I, moving from school to school was very hard at such a young age, and we dreaded it. We would enroll in a school and just when we were finally beginning to feel settled and adjusted, we would be ripped from its hallways to move to another town. This happened over and over again. Robert is three-and-a-half years younger than me, so my parents always taught me to be an example for him to calm his fears.

On entering a new school, I would try to encourage Robert. I would tell him how great this one was going to be, and how much better life was going to get for us while at the same time I was hiding my true feelings. I always tried to be a big girl, the older sister, and not show Robert that I was scared myself and wondering if things would really get better. I hated going into a classroom with all new kids staring. I felt like I was being judged the moment I stepped foot into the room. I know my experiences during these times have helped me to connect with people. I had to learn quickly how to make friends. I was kind of thrown into it, but I survived.

I believe God always had His hands protecting me because somehow, there would always be a nice girl reaching out to me to be my friend. From then on, I was okay. I would make friends very easily. Even as young as I was, I adopted a strategy to making friends. I was fairly athletic, so I would attempt to connect with others through games on the playground. I desperately wanted to be on a team, to be included. I knew that if I could just get picked onto someone's team I could really show them how fast I could run and contribute to their team. I wanted to beat everyone to the finish line. Just to hear someone say, "That girl is so fast!" was music to my ears. After I made my mark somehow, I was accepted into the group.

THE RINGING PHONES

Along with constantly changing neighborhoods and schools, my childhood was punctuated by ringing phones—non-stop! We had bill collectors calling all the time. We were at least three to four months behind on our bills. We had no access to caller ID in those days, and so we had to brace ourselves to answer all the calls so we wouldn't miss any important ones.

I remember answering the phone when I was very young. I was trained to let debt collectors know that my parents were not at home and that we were trying our hardest to pay them back. Many times the person on the other line would cuss me out because they wanted to get to my parents. I can also recall begging a collector to allow us to make $25 a month payments and hearing him refuse. I couldn't believe they weren't willing to let us pay what we could afford. The way I saw it, at least we were doing something. But, as far as the bill collectors were concerned it was all or nothing, and the badgering continued.

My parents were good, honest people just trying to survive. But these callers didn't know us and didn't care. They assumed we were just trying to dodge our bills, and were not making any effort to pay them. Many times, my dad would get on the phone with the callers to try and explain our situation and work out paying them something. Most of the time, we were not able to make it work, and so we ended up going bankrupt. I learned at an early age what this meant. We survived it, but what a long seven years it takes to get credit again once you accept bankruptcy.

HELP INDEED

In those days, our church family helped to make things a little more bearable. Whenever possible, our pastor would give us money and sometimes people in the church would drop off groceries at our doorstep. Sometimes people would give us money to help us out. A little here and a little there would somehow manage to help us stay afloat.

I was 19 years old at this point and attending Liberty Bible College in Pensacola, Florida. Dad didn't have a job, but he was looking relentlessly. He was very depressed because he couldn't make anything work. He would go for interviews, and most of the time they would tell him he was overqualified. One day I came home after college and there they were—eight paper bags of groceries. Immediately, I started digging around in one of the bags and found a tin can full of hard candy. I had not seen anything like this in a very long time. We never had the money to buy things we didn't need, only necessities. It was like I was rich with all this food. In that moment, I was just a normal kid, anticipating the first bite of candy. Everything seemed okay. That memory is very precious to me to this day.

Our life was like a roller coaster ride. One day we were living on top of the world, and then before you know it, we had lost everything that we owned. This happened many times. I often wondered if we would ever get out of this miserable life. There were days I didn't think we would make it at all. There was no hope, and no success to be found anywhere. The tide seemed to be against us as we constantly struggled to keep our heads above water.

A PIZZA PARTY

In my late teens, there was a period that we had only one car as a family, and it was in my name. Somehow we managed to keep the payments on it current. All our other cars had been repossessed by the bank. I had a job at the church working with the afterschool program. I would walk over to the school and pick up the kids, watching them until their parents got off of work. I also was the Youth Pastor for the church. I would bring home $95 a week and give it to my dad so we could buy groceries and just survive another week.

One weekend, our family planned to go out for dinner. It was nothing fancy, just an opportunity to get out as a family. We had managed to save up $17 to use for our big night out. Back then, we knew this would buy four drinks and a large pizza at Pizza Hut. Dad got his keys, and we all went out the door, looking forward to finally enjoying a good meal. However, it was not to be. When we stepped out of the house, there was no car in our parking spot. We looked everywhere around to be certain, but the car was nowhere to be found. It had been repossessed. I can recall hearing my dad say distinctly under his breath, "I knew I should have hidden the car." The sense of frustration and let down was so apparent.

It was not that Dad wasn't trying hard enough. He was. Dad was perhaps the most hardworking man I have ever known. He chased after jobs and went for interviews, but nothing seemed to work out. This was a very dark time for us. I know dad had thoughts of ending his life because he could not seem to pull us out this time. We were stuck in this horrible place in our lives. Nothing was working out, and hope was out the door. If he hadn't had the support of my mom, my brother and I, it would have been impossible to continue.

HOLDING TIGHT TO THE DREAM

For a good amount of his career, my Dad worked in Amway. He did great work for the company and got all the way to the Pearl Direct level. I am convinced that this job was pivotal in his career. He learned how to interact with others and how to make a sale. As well, it taught him to believe in himself, because no one else will if you don't. My parents were always listening to motivational audio cassette tapes in the car. And while my Dad learned about making the best life for himself, we were right there too, learning to follow our dreams. I believe hearing those motivational speakers over and over again laid the foundation for developing a positive mindset in my adulthood. Everything I heard, said, "Believe you can! Don't let anyone tell you that you are defeated!" So I was always taught that whatever I set my mind to, I could do.

When I think back to those times, there is one song that resonates in my mind. It was a song that my parents played in the car all the time titled, "Don't Let Anyone Steal Your Dream." I can still sing the chorus, and I remember singing it as a child as we drove down the road. I would sing,

Don't let anyone steal your dream, steal your dream, steal it from you. Set your goals and don't give in! Don't let anyone steal your dream and you win!

I know this may sound cheesy, but it was my life. I believed every word of it! That song summed up our life at that time. We kept trying hard to stay afloat. When many would have given up, we pushed through, knowing that someday down the road, we would get there. Our family always found a way to keep hope alive. We never gave up on each other or the future. We believed that we all have a purpose. It was just up to us to fight for it, and not to let anyone take it from us.

STAYING INSPIRED

My father loved to read inspirational books. One of his favorite authors was Zig Ziglar. Those books were a huge source of inspiration to him in those difficult times. We got used to hearing him talk to himself around the house, repeating some of Zig's inspirational lines. Also, Dad loved to quote passages from the books to us, and we grew to enjoy them perhaps as much as he did. They became a shared source of inspiration for Robert and I as we grew up and joined him in building his business.

Think and Grow Rich by Napoleon Hill was another one of Dad's favorites. That book was always next to his recliner. In our family's darkest hours, my mother would pray, and my father would sit and read books. I now know what he was doing. He was building himself up in the midst of the chaos around him. He would find wisdom and strength in those inspirational words, and he would begin again, every day, working to attain the success he knew was within arm's reach. I always knew when dad had read a chapter from one of these books. He would have a smile on his face, and he would tell us, "We are going to make it! I know we are!" That was all we needed to hear. We believed him and just knew we would come out of this dark time.

PRAYING THROUGH

In spite of all the turmoil, my parents rarely gave a clue that they were unhappy with the life we lived. Looking back, I really admire them for that. We were going through a lot, but it never seemed to get them down. Maybe they just faked it, but they acted as if their dream of living a good life was around the corner.

My parents had a very strong faith. We grew up Baptist. I can remember going to Sunday school and hearing Bible stories.

My mom grew up Pentecostal. Her dad was a traveling preacher who had a healing ministry. He wrote a book that told his life journey. I really feel that legacy has been passed down through my mom to me, as I am now writing books and carrying on his legacy.

My mom was our prayer warrior. During the down times my mom prayed, and during the up times she never stopped. She believed that if we had little, God would provide, and if we had a lot, it was all because of Him. She would pray over us each day, and those prayers clung to us through each school day. I truly believe that my mom made my dad the man he was. My parents were also giving people. Often during the hard times and in the midst of their personal need, they would still reach out and help someone else. If they had a little to give, they would give it without a second thought. Mom always made sure that we gave back. During those times when there was no money, we still tithed. It was the right thing to do.

A CITY OF CALM

And then one day, it seems like the storm stopped, and peace had finally set in. Though I waited for it to pass in the night as quickly as it had appeared, just as it had always done, this time the peace lasted. It all started the day we moved into a new home in Hattiesburg, Mississippi. This house was not a rental, but a real home we could actually feel settled in.

Dad had landed a great job at an insurance company as a regional sales manager with his own team in this city. He was great at selling insurance, so this was the perfect job. Over time, he did so well with his team that they became one of the top agencies in the nation. Dad always had great skill at selling, and his accomplishments did not go unnoticed or unrewarded. A few years later, he was recruited to join another company, and was groomed to become Vice President. Life was really good, and we seemed to finally let out the breath that we had been holding, in fear of another traumatic life change.

I was in the seventh grade when we first came to Hattiesburg. We stayed there for seven years, longer than anywhere else we had ever been, and we really put down roots. Robert and I got very involved in our church youth group and began to have somewhat of a normal life.

However, while my father continued to be more and more successful at work, his coworkers started watching him closely. As they saw it, the more business and attention he got, the less they could receive. So in an underhanded chain of events, one of his coworkers got my father fired from his job—the job that we finally thought would take care of us.

My dad made a strong effort to keep us in Hattiesburg. He immediately hit the pavement looking for work, and landed a job. Unfortunately, when my father reported to his first day of work he found out there was no longer a position for him. To this day, we still do not know what actually happened. After this disappointment, dad decided it was time to move on, no matter how much he wished he could keep his family happy in their favorite town.

REPEATING A CYCLE

I was now out of high school and working for dad. He opened up his own insurance agency, and was trying to sell insurance again. I did my best to help him, and even went as far as taking the insurance exam four times, failing each time. My heart was not in it, and I wanted no part of this up-and-down life that I had lived since third grade. But I knew I wasn't supposed to leave my family. Besides, I didn't have any money to leave. As time went on, and with Dad out of a job, we lost our house, a couple of cars, and really anything that was good in our lives was now diminishing fast. Once again we had to leave our home for a rental. So, after our brief oasis of comfortable living, we moved again, this time to the worst rental ever.

Honestly, I couldn't believe this was happening again. I mean, we had hard times from when I was in third grade all the way until my seventh grade year. I was now 19 and not ready to be part of this hard life again. I did everything I could not to follow my parents and brother to another town and rental home. After all, I was older now and had formed my own opinions of how my dad ran his life.

In my lectures and speeches, I always mention how my life was built on the side of a mountain. Quite frankly, that is no exaggeration. We literally lived on the edge, and boy did that really stress us out. It is great to take risks, but you must find balance in it. My mom was better than I would have been in how she picked up her life time and time again to follow after my dad's dreams and pursuits.[1] But we would get so mad when he would make wrong decisions. These decisions would cause the cycle of hard life circumstances to continue. He would do his best but then be sidetracked, and here we would go again. For me, this time was the final blow.

SHELVING A DREAM

I had no desire to follow my family this time. I wanted to start my own life without all the drama and hardships. As a teenager, my dream was to attend Oral Roberts University. However, at 19 when the time came for me to go to off to college, I knew there was no way I could actually do it. The family needed me desperately. So, instead of following my own dreams, I remained at home with my family and worked, doing my part to help us survive. Even though it was more difficult than I can even say, I am so glad I stayed with my family. They needed me, and I needed them. We were a family of four who clung to each other because we were all we had.[2]

Lesson 1: Consider Your Support Systems. One important thing you must have to succeed is a strong support system. As you push towards your dreams, make sure to take into consideration those around you so you don't lose them in your pursuit. Be sure those around you have the capacity to take the journey with you.

Lesson 2: Family Is Special. We can go out and change the world and still end up leaving our families behind. But I believe that taking time to take care of our own is the most valuable thing we can do. It can also be the hardest thing ever. Many times our family might take us for granted, since we are 'just family.' But I knew I was supposed to be there with and for my family, despite my desire to be other places, and so I stuck it out. Be a support to your family. It will go a long way.

This became one of the lowest points of our lives. We were quickly drowning again, repeating the past that we thought we had escaped from. Not one thing would open up for us. This was when I got my own job to help support the family, bringing home $95 a week. Again, we only had one car that had not been taken by the bank. We scraped by every week on the little money I made.

THE STRENGTH OF A WOMAN

According to Mom, Dad felt completely defeated because we were behind on payments for everything, and we were drowning in debt. He would get up defeated and many times go to bed defeated. If not for my mom, I am sure my dad would not have pulled through. I can remember my mom encouraging him constantly. She would always tell him how great he was, and that he was a winner.

I am sure Mom's prayers and encouragement worked because during those times of deep struggle, somehow, Dad would always emerge with a new dream or passion to move us forward. My dad was an entrepreneur that would never give up, and Mom was like a boxer's corner-man at the ringside, cleaning his bleeding nose, giving him water and encouraging him to get back into the ring and fight. Because my mom didn't throw in the towel, Dad won, and the whole family came into a better place.[3]

This financial crisis in my family lasted for several more years. In those days, I did my best to help my family stay positive. When my brother was in his senior year of high school we all tried to be upbeat for him so he could enjoy this important time of life. One thing we always did was celebrate. Even though life was not shining very brightly for us we knew how to laugh, and when we had a little extra money, we would buy some dip and chips and have our own little party. Laughter is indeed the best medicine. It helped to soften the impact of the hard falls we experienced along the way.

Lesson 3: Your Support Can't Give Up. If you are going to win the game of life, you need to make sure you are surrounded by people who will not give up on you even when you mess up.

THE TURNAROUND

Beyond laughter, there was much prayer and faith. That was not an option. We prayed, believed and we hoped against hope that one day there would be a turnaround. Life pressed us hard and our struggle intensified, but we grew closer and stronger as a family, and so did our faith until finally there was a breakthrough. It didn't look like much at the time, but it was the beginning of the end of that long drought.

Dad started a business with a friend from church—an environmental and safety compliance company. The business began to do well, and Dad eventually bought the business from his partner. It soon became a family affair, with all of us working different jobs for the company. My mom was a huge motivator, and she helped as much as possible.

Dad knew nothing about environmental and safety regulations, much less how to keep a business in compliance with OSHA and the EPA. But he began to read article after article to become informed on this industry. His exceptional memory came in handy as he read manuals, regulations and became an expert in this emerging field. According to my mom, he told her that he asked God to help him retain information, and God did! He was his own boss, his own teacher and the only one who was accountable for the things that happened to us from that point on. And surprisingly, in the midst of this chaos, our story began to change.

CASH FLOW

We slowly started to create a cash flow with the new business. Eventually, we were able to purchase a blue Chevy truck and our first video camera. I will never forget the day my dad went to a video rental company to ask them if he could buy a video camera and pay monthly payments. This camera would be used to video my dad as he did presentations on safety and environmental compliance. The owner said yes, and the rest is history.

The business required travel. Dad would set up a meeting with body shop owners in a town like Huntsville, AL. He would drive up to meet them in the evening and attempt to sell our company's services. For a one-time fee, our company would offer these businesses the services and documentation needed to bring their operations into compliance with OSHA and EPA regulations, and then we would keep them up-to-date for a monthly service fee.

A CRY OF DESPERATION

I will never forget the day Dad called me while I was at work. This was 1990, and cell phones were just coming out. Calling someone on a cell phone was usually reserved for an emergency. As I answered his call, Dad said, "Baby, tell your mama to pray for me. I only have enough money to get to Huntsville. I have to make a sale, or I won't have the money to get home." Tears rolled down my cheeks, because it seemed we were always teetering on the edge of hopelessness. I thought, *"God please, please help us get through this. I don't want to go backwards. We have come so far, and we need this one breakthrough."*

I hung up the phone and called Mom. I can remember just putting my head in my hands and asking out loud in desperation, "Couldn't anything ever just come through for us?" Once again, we were in dire straits. But, I was encouraged by the fact that my dad was such a great salesman, and I knew that if he set his mind to it, he could get at least one of those business owners to come aboard with us. Plus, I knew that if God was for us, who can be against us?

THE HOME RUN

About 10 o'clock at night Dad called and said he had sold a company package to all 12 of the body shop owners. We hit a home run! That night, he slept in the truck in Huntsville, then woke up and cashed the new checks so he could get home. He didn't mind the uncomfortable sleeping arrangements because he could recognize the victory, and through his perseverance he felt that he was finally ending up on top.

The safety compliance company began to expand and grow. As time went on, Dad saw the need for training and education in the safety and environmental field. He decided to create a certificate program that was designed to teach a small business owner how to bring his own business into compliance. Over time, the popularity of the certificate program grew more than we ever expected. Robert, my brother, and Tommy, my husband, helped Dad with this new expansion. They wrote some of the curriculum and it became very successful.

A NEAR TRAGEDY

Things were finally starting to look up. We had gotten on our feet, and now we actually had a chance to take a vacation. It had been years since we had taken one, and so our anticipation was high. Dad booked us on our first cruise, and it was only a day away when our lives could have taken a very wrong turn.

Mom and I had just returned from shopping for clothes for the cruise. Dad wasn't there, but we knew he would be coming home shortly. He had been out riding the four-wheeler in our neighborhood, waiting for us to come home. Mom and I went into our rooms to start packing. We were all busy and excited about going on the cruise the next day. Suddenly, I heard a loud popping sound outside. It was like a huge piece of plastic had been broken. I looked out my window, which faced the country road in front of our house, and I saw my dad lying down in the middle of the road.

Immediately, I started screaming and calling out to my mom, as I went flying out of my room. I jumped a 4-foot rail to get to the front door. I was terrified of what I would find as I approached the road. The first thing I saw was a car to my left, down in a ditch, and Dad's four-wheeler on the other side of the road completely destroyed. Putting two and two together, I knew then that Dad's four-wheeler had been hit by a car. Dad was lying on the ground with his eyes closed. His sunglasses were broken and hanging loose on his face. I couldn't see any blood, but he was just lifeless and that scared me.

I knelt beside him, and began to call to him, "Wake up! Dad! Dad!" At the same time, I was praying and believing that he was not dead. As soon as I called out to him to come back to life, he woke up. His eyes opened and he said, "What happened, baby?"

At about this time, a woman who was a nurse came to help, and someone else who had seen what happened called for an ambulance. My mom and I continued to pray over him as we awaited the paramedics. Robert arrived while Dad was still lying on the ground. Everyone agreed it was a miracle he was alive and talking to us.

The paramedics took Dad to the hospital and immediately into surgery. He had a broken jaw, his arm was broken and needed pins put in it. Other than that, he was a miracle. Of course, since we had no insurance and no money to pay hospital bills (still in the early days of our business), he was shortly sent home to recover, in a portable hospital bed. My mom nursed him back to health, and after about two months he was up and around, even coming back to work.

This was a season of breakthrough and financial blessing, but things were still very tenuous. We were still mostly on a shoestring budget, and my dad's accident very nearly derailed our company entirely. Fortunately, God protected Dad even in the accident, and our company was able to continue. We did not get to go on our dream vacation, but we had Dad with us, strong and healthy again, and that was all that mattered.

BUILDING A LEGACY

Dad wasn't content with the limited success he had achieved. We had found some financial stability, but Dad continued to dream even bigger. Dad had a vision to start an educational institution that would offer the safety certificate program we had created along with degrees in occupational safety and environmental management. The programs would be offered via correspondence to meet the needs of adult learners.

This is yet another experience I can never forget. The family gathered together one day, and my Dad announced, "We are going to start a university." I thought to myself, *"Are you serious? After all we have been through, we are now going into education?"* I questioned it for a few seconds, and then I thought, *"Why not? Let's do it; I am in!"* Tommy, Robert, my mom, me and a few others agreed, and we all went back to work. What a dream! We chose the name of our college at our family table. We first named it University of Environmental Sciences, but later we picked the final name for the university, Columbia Southern University (CSU), which has stuck to this day. I will never forget that day nor did I really understand the impact our college would truly make.

Through hard work, working with experts in the field, regulatory approvals and more, the institution was launched. It started very slowly, and at first it was funded by our safety consultant company. The rest of the family thought Dad was a little crazy to go into the education business. Growing the school was not easy. It required significant work to establish. Our main strategy was to take great care of our students, and as a result they would refer others. After approximately six years of operation, we applied to become accredited. This proved to be harder than we ever dreamed, but we were driven to succeed.

At one point, I remember Dad and Mom taking a second mortgage on their home to keep the business afloat. To reduce payroll cost, we began to close at 3:00 PM on Fridays, reducing the work week to 38 hours instead of 40 for all employees. There were many weeks when the family would take no pay at all. My brother Robert and Dr. Joe Manjone were an integral part of the accreditation process. It was a struggle, but they made it happen. After approximately eight years of operations, we were formally accredited. This was a pivotal point in the school's history. While we had hoped enrollments would jump as a result of this monumental effort, growth continued slowly for some time. We worked tirelessly to make sure every component of the student experience was positive and continuously improved every aspect of the institution.

As we watched the certificate program grow, we knew we had to offer more. Believing that education was part of our legacy, we began to offer even more degree programs. This was a difficult time for the young university, and there were even times that we almost folded, but we kept moving forward. The university began to grow, and now it has become one of the top online universities in the nation. The family has continued its involvement in the school, and each year we have added more and more excellent team members to help us take it to the next level.

THE BATON IS PASSED

In 2005, CSU reached 7,000 students. This was also the year my father unexpectedly became ill. Dad had always had good health, and so we never imagined that his sickness would result in him staying in the hospital for five months and eventually passing away at the age of 60. It was shocking how fast his health declined. I honestly thought we would have him with us for a while longer, but we soon realized it was now up to us to move the university forward.

My brother Robert, who was 33 at the time, stepped up and took over as President of CSU. Robert had run the operations of the school under Dad, but this new role would also require him to focus externally into new business development and strategic relationship building. He had understudied Dad and prepared himself, so I knew he would be very successful in leading the university to another level. As usual, all the family stepped up to more responsibility and rallied behind Robert while at the same time dealing with the loss of Dad. Our staff and faculty were also very dedicated to keeping the school moving forward.

Now, 11 years since Dad passing, CSU has grown from 7,000 students to over 29,000, with over 60,000 alumni. Due to the growth of the school and its need for our focus, the safety consulting company was sold to my uncle. It still thrives today. When Dad passed, there were those who thought that we children would never be able to take the reins of the organization. But they were wrong. Not only have we maintained it, we have also grown it, because we were well prepared.

Looking at where we came from and comparing it to where we are now, my family is truly a miracle. It was only God who could bring a family from as difficult a situation as we were in to such a place of success and honor. Out of all those hard times we experienced, our passion and legacy emerged—education.[4] We can relate to the struggles of others because we have been through it. We understand that feeling of hopelessness that casts a shadow on every dream and aspiration, and that is

---

Lesson 4: Find Your Passion. Often your passion emerges from hard times. What you have gone through in your past and the way you managed to persevere through it become the driving force enabling you to help others. If you have lost your passion, I am sure it's not far away. Look behind you to see what has caused you to emerge in life, and usually your passion is close by.

why we believe in learning. Education is powerful. It's a tool, a ticket to a fresh start and a new life. Offering education to adult learners, as a means of moving forward in their careers, brings hope to many who otherwise would be stuck. That's why we're still passionate about it today.

TAKING IT FURTHER

In 2010, a second institution, Waldorf College, located in Forest City, Iowa, was added to the organization. We have given it a face lift and rebranded it as Waldorf University to reflect its new mission. It has huge potential with both an on-campus program and online. For us as a family, our vision is to change lives through education and make a difference in each student we serve, and we continue to do that through both CSU and Waldorf University.

We were the family most unlikely to succeed. But we did, and we never want to forget where we came from. Through all the growth and expansion we have experienced over the years as a family and a business, we have kept one relic from the past: the old blue Chevy truck that Dad traveled with and slept in the night he closed his breakthrough deal. We kept *Ol' Blue* to remind us of where we came from and where God has brought us.[5]

THERE'S A WAY OUT

Our life story is a testimony that proves you must never lose sight of your dream. If you never give up, you will win. My parents hung in there, in the face of impossible situations, and they pushed through.

Lesson 5: Don't Forget Your Roots And Your Story. Sometimes the journey into success can be so painful that once you reach the top, you don't want any remembrance of the past and its shame. However, being mindful of the past helps us to keep our life in perspective. For our family, remembering our story helps us to be grateful and to stay humble.

With faith in God and the sheer determination to just go for it, we overcame enormous obstacles and fulfilled our dreams. We also can now help others with their dreams.[6]

When you are down and feeling hopeless, the littlest challenge can look like a huge mountain. However, there is always a way out of every situation. This is what my family has adopted as a slogan: When faced with problems or impossible situations, you can go through the mountain, go around the mountain, go over the mountain, or simply pick that mountain up and move it out of your way.[7]

With just a snapshot of my family's story, I believe that whatever difficult situation you find yourself in, you too can find hope. We are all going through one thing or another, but what counts is how the story ends. For some, your story is just beginning, and for others, you are in the middle and struggling to make it to the finish line. I know one thing; if we made it, so can you!

Lesson 6: Just Push Through. I know my kids get tired of hearing me say this, because I say it at least once a week! There are going to be those dreaded times when you just don't want to deal with anything. It might take everything inside of you to face your situation and just make it through it. As long as you don't stop moving forward, you are winning! But the minute you stop, you are setting yourself up for failure. Keep pushing through the hard times. Remember—just keep moving forward.

Lesson 7: Go Through The Mountains Of Life. Just because someone says you can't succeed at something doesn't mean you go down without a fight! When someone says, "You can't do it," that just gets me fired up. "Yes I can!" In the early days, people laughed and snickered at my parents for having the vision to start a college. Most people never believed in them. But my parents didn't let it defeat them. In the same way, you can't let discouragement get you down. Sometimes, you have to go against all odds and just make it happen. Go through your mountains—they aren't as big as they seem!

Chapter 2

NEW BEGINNINGS

Champions are not made in a day and their paths are not the easiest to walk. Have you been laboring and pushing for success, only to find yourself asking, *'Why is it taking so long?'* Or the more familiar, *'Why is it so difficult?'* Take heart, you are not the only one. Many successful people have shared a similar experience. Don't forget, this is not the end, and in fact, there's hope for your future.

PROCESS YOUR SUCCESS

There is no question that it can be quite frustrating when you have so much potential, work hard and yet feel stuck, unable to make headway in life. I saw that with my parents firsthand, and I have experienced it for myself as well. It is definitely not pleasant. However, the real danger is missing the opportunities for learning and personal growth that those tough seasons in life can offer. Allowing yourself the space to go through those tough times and knowing that there are major lessons to learn as you go through them will, I hope, make those seasons a little more understandable and profitable. I call this time, "The Process." It is during this time that you learn the most, and it is how you walk through the process that determines your future success.

JUMPING THROUGH HOOPS

Long before I would become part owner and an executive of two colleges, and sit in meetings with some of the top corporate executives in the nation, I was just Chantell—a young girl playing basketball in Mississippi. There were only two things going for me: a strong faith and a feisty desire to succeed.

During the four years I played on the girls' basketball team, I went through some of the most challenging and grueling experiences of my youth. However, those would become some of the most formative and fruitful years of my life. I developed a tough skin—the ability to endure trials and to keep going after my dreams even when there are delays and demotions. I learned how to be disciplined, work under leadership and in a team environment. I would get up every day, tired and weary, and still make it to practice. Above all, I learned how to be a leader—to be led and to lead others. My time on the basketball team taught me to push through the pain and disappointments that come with life, and literally prepared me to be a success. It is this season of my life that I reflect on most often even to this day. I gain insight from those times to help me lead myself and others.

From the locker room to the game court, and even in the stands, the sports world is filled with many valuable life lessons for those who will pay close attention. Life is certainly not a game, but it is like sports in the sense that it is governed by important rules. If you want to win in the game of life, you must learn, master and apply these rules. I am glad and honored to share some of these important life lessons with you. My hope is that it will inspire you to push toward success, as it did for me.

DESPERATE FOR CHANGE

When I was 13 years old, my family moved to Hattiesburg, Mississippi into the Oak Grove Community School district. We had gone through repeated financial hardships and were desperate for change.[8] My dad was starting a new job as an insurance agent in this town, and so it seemed like this could be a new start for our whole family. Lord knows, we needed a new beginning, and yes, for the umpteenth time![9]

Lesson 8: You Must Be Desperate For Change. If you want a new beginning, you must be dissatisfied enough with where you are to want to get out. There has to be something in you that wants more in life and will not accept things as they are. You must be willing to fight to be more. Be determined not to settle for average, and always strive to be above average. You must have a dream, and be desperate about making that dream a reality.

Lesson 9: Don't Be Afraid To Start Again And Again. Imagine if a child learning to walk stopped trying after falling for the fifth

Though there was nothing in this particular move that promised anything new or different from previous ones, it was a door of opportunity, and we took it. Whether it was going to be a successful place for my family, we didn't know, and maybe we didn't care. But it promised a new beginning and that was enough. Sometimes the best you can hope for is change.

During those years of moving from one city to another and shuffling through multiple schools, I learned to embrace change. I was so used to change that I actually looked forward to it. I began to hope that something might be better than it was before.[10] I am sure that is why today I handle change with anticipation of good things coming my way.

The school we attended before the move was huge; a real big-city high school. It had about 1500 students in a two-story building. In so many ways, it was a very hard school to attend. You could easily get lost in the crowd. For me, trying to fit in was rather hard. I could never seem to find the right kind of

---

time because she is embarrassed, tired or says to herself, 'This walking thing is too difficult!' She would miss out on everything the future holds for her.

It's okay to start over. You may have to restart with something else, but you must never stop trying. Never give up. My parents never stopped believing they would make it out of poverty. Even though we went bankrupt and people were telling them they would never amount to anything, they still believed in their dream. It doesn't matter how many times you fail, but what does matter is how fast you get back up.

Lesson10: Embrace Change. *The truth is, change will happen. It's your choice to avoid it or embrace it. Learning that change was good was probably the best gift I could have ever received. One of the obstacles that leaders face most often is their ability to handle change. Many times people are thrown off track when change comes at them. The best leaders learn to accept change and go with it. The quicker you embrace it, the quicker things seem to fall in place.*

friends to connect with. Looking back, I wonder how I was able to survive there at all.

On the other hand, this new school in Hattiesburg was exactly the opposite. It was more laidback, with just about 150 students housed in a much smaller building. The kids were friendly and accepting, and I knew I could actually make friends here. I felt more at home in this school than at any other school I had attended before, and that helped me become more hopeful about life and our family's future.[11]

FINDING A NICHE

Robert Jr. and I started school in the middle of the year. We both were excited and, at the same time, scared about the prospect of another school yet again. We knew the drill, oh so well—walking into a classroom with every eye on you as you made your way to your seat. But we were happy to be there, and we looked forward to new friends and a new life. Robert had other interests, but I intended to join the school band. I was hoping to make new friends and improve my musical skills at the same time. So I was shocked to learn that all the spots on the school band had been filled since the beginning of the year. We were just too late. I couldn't believe that there were no spots open anywhere for me.

For a while I thought that my only hope for fitting into the culture of the school was gone for at least another year, or perhaps even forever if, God forbid, we moved again. However, my mom encouraged me to look closer. There had to be other

---

Lesson 11: Adapt To Your Environment. Changing jobs or attending a new school always has its anxious moments. But even in these moments, keep an open mind—listen and learn. Give those new environments a chance to grow on you. And if you will stay optimistic as you face new challenges, you will be able to adapt to even the most challenging environments.

opportunities.[12] Even though I was very disappointed, I began to explore other options for extracurricular activities, without much hope of a solution. It wasn't too long into my search that I heard that basketball tryouts were in the spring of that year. Exciting! Apparently, not all doors were closed.

These tryouts offered an opportunity to be on the Junior Varsity girls' basketball team. Fortunately, I have always been athletic and have played many sports. I have run track and won many races because I was a very fast runner. However, I had never really looked at basketball or considered it seriously, even though both of my parents had played basketball in high school.[13] It was a most unexpected turn of events, and I had to think about it for a few days. But I needed to make up my mind quickly if I wanted to take advantage of this opportunity.

TAKING A CHANCE

My mom encouraged me to just go for it. Who knows, I just might make the team. I didn't have much experience with basketball, but I was determined to be chosen for the team.

Lesson 12: When One Door Shuts, Look For Another. Just because one dream dies, that does not mean you give up. Usually, when one door shuts, another one opens, but you have to be looking to find it. So always keep your eyes open for other positions and opportunities, and you will be surprised by what you find.

Lesson 13: You Have Hidden Talents And Gifts. My parents both played basketball in high school; it was definitely imprinted on my DNA. It was possible that I could be good at it too, but I had never thought about it before. If there was a spot on the band, I wouldn't have cared about basketball tryouts or the team. I would've been very content in the band throughout high school, and never realized what I had missed—the chance to be a champion.

You may also have a game changer, an ace up your sleeve, that you may not know about. In the game of life, that gives you a fighting chance, a chance for success. We often only realize it when we find ourselves in a tight corner or dire straits. Use that time to dig deeper and find that hidden talent.

Even though I didn't know much about the sport, I didn't let fear keep me from just getting out and trying it.[14] For one thing, I knew I could use speed to my advantage at the tryouts. I started practicing immediately.[15] Most afternoons, I would go outside and practice dribbling by myself.[16] Dad bought a basketball goal for our driveway, to help me learn how to shoot the ball and make a lay-up, both of which were requirements for the tryout.

I had the best coaching in the world. My parents had played basketball in high school, so they both gave me advice and coached me when they had time. My dad had me running sprints, shooting baskets and doing lay-ups.

I wanted this so bad, and I was willing to put in whatever time it took to be ready for the big day. Making the team was all I could think about. I thought, *'This is my chance to make my mark, to be known and fit in.'* I just had to make it onto the team. [17]

Lesson 14: Try Something New. Don't be afraid to try something new and different. Too often, we get stuck in our ways and are afraid to attempt new things even though the old is not working. Don't get caught in that trap!

Lesson 15: Give it Your Best Shot. I had never played basketball before, but it was the only door open for me. I was determined to give it a shot. No, my best shot. If you must give something a try, go all in, and give it your best. That's the only way to realize its full potential.

Lesson 16: You Must Pay The Price For Success. How badly do you want it? Take time to evaluate how much time you need to put into your dreams to be successful. Making the effort to get additional training could be the thing that gets you that new job or position on the team. You have to desire it so much that you do what it takes to succeed. For me, nothing came easy. I always had to go the extra mile to be successful.

Lesson 17: Utilize Your Resources. You may be very gifted, skilled and have a lot of experience, but that doesn't mean that you should

Learning to make a lay-up proved very hard for me. I had trouble dribbling and looking up at the right time to shoot. My timing was off, and I got very frustrated. But I knew I needed to master these techniques before the tryout day. I was absolutely certain that I would not be the only one trying to find a spot on the team.[18]

Next, I had to master dribbling with both hands while running. I had no problem running, but I would run so fast that I would leave the ball behind. When I ran track, there was no demand on me to run with a ball. But in basketball that is done constantly, and I needed to learn how to apply my running skills appropriately in this new game. At the same time I was adapting my old skills, I had to learn completely new ones. It was quite a challenge. I had to focus on both elements and take my time with practicing each skill.

I wished I had more time to practice, but time was a luxury, and the tryouts were approaching very quickly. One thing I was sure of concerning the tryouts was that I could run fast and possibly beat all the others who were participating. So with little time to practice, I had to hone in on that talent and hope everything else would fall into place.

---

go it on your own or do it all by yourself. Instead, you have to learn to utilize the help of people around you, like I did with my parents. They coached me and offered me the emotional and psychological boost I needed to succeed at the tryouts. You may not have it all— but someone you know has just what you need!

Lesson 18: There's Always Competition. No matter how small the stakes may be, whether it's about getting onto a high school basketball team, winning a date or getting that job you've been dreaming of, there's always someone else who also wants to win that prize. Remembering that is key to pushing yourself into excellence. Yes, it may have only been the basketball team of a small high school, but my spot was not guaranteed. There were others who were also pushing hard to earn their spot.

On the morning of the tryouts, my mom sent me out with words of encouragement. "You are going to make the team, and you have it within you to become the best player on the team. You've worked hard, and it's going to pay off."[19] By the time I walked out the door I felt like I could conquer just about anything and win! I prayed so hard, asking God to guide my every move when I had the ball and to help me make my shots. Even at that early stage, I could see myself playing on the team with my new teammates.[20]

The tryouts were very intense and challenging for me, both physically and emotionally. I didn't know any of the other girls or have a personal connection with the coach. Everything

---

Lesson 19: Use Your Exceptional Qualities. *Hone in on what you are good at, rather than what you aren't good at. For me, I was a very fast runner. I felt that might be just enough for me to make the basketball team. I may not have been good at basketball, but that wasn't going to stop me. When I tried out, I wasn't the best dribbler or the best shot. However, I was faster than anyone else. I could be taught how to dribble and shoot later on.*

During a job interview, a tryout or a pitch, always find a way to showcase that exceptional quality about you. It just might make the difference. You may not be good at everything needed in a job or position you are seeking, but you do have something to offer. So make it count. Don't let what you don't have blind you to what you can do.

Lesson 20: Go In Like A Champion. *If you practice very hard for a tryout, an interview or a pitch, but go in feeling defeated, there is no way you can come out on top. You have to have your mind set that you are already a winner. You might be nervous (that's okay!), but you have to see yourself on top and winning.*

You see, it's not just about the skill; the attitude counts. Whether you are fully prepared or not, when the time comes, go in with confidence. My mom made sure that I went into the tryout without any doubts about my abilities or chances. And that confidence made all the difference.

was new to me—the coach, the players, the court and even the game. The only thing familiar was the ball. Once or twice, I thought about going back home. But this was not the time to look back. I ran my heart out during warm ups and speed tests, and tried my hardest to focus on my dribbling and lay-ups. I did all I knew to do, to the utmost of my ability, and trusted that would be enough.[21]

A BIG WIN

After a few agonizing days of waiting, the roster was posted, and I had made the freshman team. Wow! I was so excited that day. I finally felt like I fit in. After all the schools I had been to, I finally felt at home.[22] My family took me out for a burger to celebrate. My journey into basketball had just started. I had not won a single game, any championships or titles. My family was still not where we wanted to be financially.

Lesson 21: Leave It All On The Table. Sometimes in life you may get a second chance at the same opportunity. But most of the time, you only have one shot. That means you have to make every moment count. You have to leave it all on the table. When you are done, let there be no regrets. Don't let it be said of you that you could have done better if only you had tried harder. When I participated in the basketball tryouts, I brought my best game. That's how I secured a spot on the team.

Lesson 22: Just Go For It. You will never know unless you give it a try. Being scared of the unknown is healthy as long as you don't let it defeat you. Take chances; you might actually make it! I was not good at basketball, but I was good at running. Nothing else was available for me at the time, so I went for it. Maybe you are at a crossroads and are scared of the unknown. It could be a position, job or an opening on a team, and you are scared you won't make it. Remember, you will never know if you don't try.

But I had gotten a victory that was worth celebrating, and so we made it a point to do just that.[23]

Lesson 23: Take Time To Celebrate Victories And Special Moments.
Even if you are not where you want to be in life and find yourself uncertain about the future, there will always be an opportunity to celebrate. It may be a small victory or a special occasion, but take the time to celebrate. Having a spirit of gratitude makes the tough parts of the journey bearable. It gives you a positive outlook on life and makes it worth living.

Chapter 3

DEVELOPING A CHAMPION

Perhaps there has never been a longer summer than the one preceding my first semester on the basketball team. All throughout that summer, I could imagine my teammates and I playing other teams as my family and friends cheered for me on the sidelines. Several times a week, I would ask my parents about their experiences playing on their high school teams. The game of basketball had become the most exciting thing in my life, filling me with hope at a very difficult time in my life.

PRACTICE, PRACTICE, PRACTICE

Finally, the school year started, and basketball practice was in full swing. I was pumped up and ready to go! I had been dreaming of it all summer and just could not wait any longer. I was so excited as I walked to my first practice, looking forward to meeting my teammates and shooting some hoops. That day, right after class, I was out the door and headed for the gym. I was probably the first player to get there, and I felt so proud of it. I was on the basketball team.

My first coach was Coach Bean. He was kind but firm. He took his job seriously and was determined to make champions out of us. From the beginning, it became very clear to me that I would have to work very hard and earn every bit of playing time.[24]

Lesson 24: Earn Your Spot. Live and work in such a way that people who would otherwise not be kind to you, have no option but to consider you above others. When you find yourself in a group and everyone is new, realize that you are all on the same level, with the same potential and opportunities. Your next step will be to show that you have what it takes to make it to the next level. Go at it with everything you have because nothing worth

To be clear, I was not one to be lazy. I had labored tirelessly preparing for the tryouts, but I knew I was going to have to put in a lot more effort during practice in order to make the first string roster.[25]

I started my basketball career in the ninth grade on the Junior Varsity team. As I had very little experience playing the game, JV was the perfect fit for me. It was rather reassuring to know that I was not the only newbie on the team. Perhaps that is one great thing about starting a sport at a young age; everyone is still learning the game and striving to master the fundamentals, making it easier to participate. I felt like I belonged, and even better, I didn't feel daunted or less than the others. I knew I was capable of taking on the challenge of learning this new sport and that attitude helped me meet my coach's expectations.[26]

having will come easy. I never wanted anything just handed to me. I wanted to earn it so that no one could take it away from me. I did, and you can too.

If you expect everything to be easy it won't be worth fighting for. Go into every experience as an opportunity to learn and gather information that might come in handy in the future along your journey. It might not be what you are looking for, but it has fallen into your path. Go with it, and see what happens.

Lesson 25: Be A Hard Worker. *You must develop a very strong work ethic, because there is no such thing as opportunity without work. Once you go through an open door you will have to work even harder to take full advantage of it. Be ready at all times to take on whatever life might throw at you.*

Work hard, work smart and be at work on time. Work through challenges and difficulties because hard work always pays off. At a very young age I took on those hard times as a personal challenge. I was not about to let anything conquer me. Because I stuck it out, it helped me later in life to get to where I am today.

Lesson 26: Be Very Confident. *Be confident in your abilities and skills. As you start to work at a job or position you have landed, you must do it with confidence. Always hold your head up high, believing in yourself and your ability to execute that office.*

Practices began a few weeks after school started, and so we had a good six to eight weeks to get ready for our first game. We would hit the court every day after school, practicing until the sun went down. We did chest passes and learned to dribble the ball without looking at it. Sprinting was a huge part of the routine. We would have multiple sprinting sessions to develop speed. Coach Bean would often say to us, "If you don't have the basics down, in the long run, you are not going to be a star player!" So he pushed us hard every day, and we practiced the basics over and over again.

During the first few weeks, we really didn't scrimmage at all or do anything very intense. It was all about learning and capitalizing on the basics of the game. In later weeks, the coach took it up a notch, adding advanced training and conditioning routines. I will never forget running bleachers over and over again. I truly thought my legs were going to fall off.[27]

There are times when I feel inadequate and unready for a particular responsibility. It may even be to the point where unconsciously I am allowing fear to settle in and paralyze me. When I catch myself, I snap out of it and tell myself, "Chantell, you can do this. You've made it this far; you can do this." So I psych myself up, change my attitude and start working it. Confidence is essential.

Lesson 27: You Can Take It. *We all want to stay in our comfort zones. For instance when we embrace the need for rigorous training or exercise, there is a certain level of reluctance about how much we think we can do or how far we think we can go. But the truth is we can all go that extra mile. You have the ability to push yourself past your limits. You can tap into hidden resources and inner strength to get over any hurdle. If you have a personal fitness or weight loss goal, believe that you can push yourself to accomplish it and you will.*

Don't allow yourself to quit something prematurely. It might feel hard to you, but that is the reason to push through it. Remember that you are growing and maturing. If you can follow through, this tenacity you are developing will be something that you will carry with you the rest of your life.

Practice was exciting at the beginning, but it had some significant challenges. After a while, it began to lose its luster and take its toll.[28] I cannot count the number of times I fell, made a poor pass or failed to make a basket. Often I would come home sore and bruised, feeling like I could never go to practice again.

Even for a young girl, life felt very difficult at those times and often, as I drifted off to sleep, I wanted to close my eyes and wish it all away. I used to wonder why everything had to be so hard for me. I would look at others and wish I could have it as easy as them. I would constantly say to my parents, "Why is everything so hard in life?" But I knew this was just another opportunity to learn and to push myself forward.[29]

I could definitely feel the emotional strain of it all. Having to push myself so hard to make the team had its drawbacks. In addition, changing schools over seven times was finally taking a toll on me. As I began to fall in love with my team, the fear of

_____

Lesson 28: Focus On The Big Picture. *Anytime you start something new, it feels fresh and exciting. You are sure you can meet the challenge. But somewhere in the middle, reality hits. You might even begin to wonder, 'What have I gotten myself into?' This is the time to keep moving forward, even though it's exhausting, by focusing on the end result—the big picture. After all, "When the going gets tough, the tough get going."*

Lesson 29: Be Determined To Overcome Difficulties. *Every level of success comes with its own challenges, but you must make an effort to push past them and not allow them to slow your momentum. There were difficulties I overcame when I tried out for the basketball team. And after I made the cut, I faced a different set of challenges that I had to choose to overcome as well.*

Life is about learning and going through new challenges. They will always be there so you have to have the right attitude to take them on. If you don't, you will find yourself coming right back to the same challenge over and over again. Always take the challenge and go with it. The experience you are gaining is so valuable to your future.

losing this beautiful experience was real. I can remember many nights my mom would come into my room before bed and just sit and listen to my frustrations. She would always give me some great advice that would pick me back up, and let me fall asleep with a renewed sense of hope.

The next day, after a full night's rest, I would feel rejuvenated and ready to get back on the court. At the beginning of practice, you would find me running with a limp from sore muscles as I warmed up. But pretty soon, all the pain would be forgotten as I rushed and hustled after the ball, dribbling to the basket. I was always determined to push through the pain no matter what.[30] Regardless of how I felt physically or emotionally, I always made sure to give my best during practice.[31]

Lesson 30: Learn To Rest. When you have worked hard, you must take time to rest. You've earned it. Learn to rest physically and mentally. It's not enough to stop physical activity; you also need to lay down the burdens in your mind and your heart. Sometimes the key to overcoming a difficult situation is rest and not more activity. In addition to giving your body and mind that needed break, rest helps to give you a clearer picture of your situation. Choosing to rest on a daily and weekly basis will help you refresh, reset and make you ready for the next task. If we are a part of a team, we owe it to the team to rest and be at our best for everyone.

Lesson 31: No Excuses Whatsoever. Don't allow your frustrations to get the better of you, and don't let your emotional or physical pain interfere with your relationships or your performance. If you take a closer look at yourself and your circumstances, you can find every excuse and justification to just lie in bed and refuse to take another step. Instead, choose not to excuse or justify yourself.

I allow myself to have those "poor me moments" or pity parties for just a short time. After I have cried or voiced my frustrations out loud, I give myself a few minutes to an hour or so, and then I move on. It is so important to be real with yourself and to take time to just vent, but then you have got to get back up and move forward. Many times, it is not going to be fair as you play the game of life. It is how you deal with those moments that determine if you have the makings of a champion.

What helped me was remembering that feeling and surge of emotions when I hit the mark. Winning always feels great, and that feeling I knew very well. I would constantly replay memories of winning races in track and even further back to other successes. I never forgot those experiences, and so I always played to win! These memories kept me going in hard times.

While practicing for basketball, I also had to keep up with my school work and grades. This was perhaps the hardest part of it all—going back and forth between the seemingly opposing roles of academics and athletics as I juggled all my various responsibilities. My grades were average during my high school years. I played all four years, at any sport I could try out for. Balancing homework and sports was always a challenge because all I would dream about was winning a game.

I always had to study harder because I just couldn't catch on the first few times. While my friends would seem to understand a subject so easily, it would take me reviewing a subject over and over again before I could really understand the concept or remember what I read. When I took the time and applied myself, I always received good grades. Schoolwork was just another challenge, and I had to be ready to take my homework more seriously and really put time into it. I knew education was important. It had to be my priority if I wanted to be able to play sports, and of course, to make it into college.[32]

Lesson 32: Learn To Balance Your Responsibilities. *Finding a balance in everything you do is an ongoing job. Putting sports ahead of academics was an area I always struggled with, but it was necessary. We can get out of balance easily, and if we don't pay attention to this on a weekly basis, we can lose valuable time that we could have used to advance toward our goals in life.*

Stay in check each week. Be sure you know what your priorities are, and put them first. Making education a priority is essential at whatever stage you are in life. It is after high school that you really start to understand the value of your education. Moreover, most jobs that are career-oriented require some form of specialized education. Going back to college can be done at whatever age you are at. I often say, "Education will help you find your purpose."

TEAM PLAYER
Basketball is a team sport, and so in addition to improving my individual skill, I had to master how to play on a team.[33] It is one thing to be good at the elements of a sport, and it is another to be able to play with a group of people and be coached.[34]

Lesson 33: It Takes A Team. *Individual talents and skills do not win championships—great and disciplined teams do. You must see yourself as part of a team. There are others who are supposed to play a role in your success and vice versa. It's okay to feel as though, 'I can't do this all by myself,' and it's okay to seek help. You can't do it all, and in fact, you're not supposed to.*

In real life, there is no such thing as a lone wolf. Going it alone is dangerous. Being a team player and understanding the role of others is of utmost importance as you move forward in life. Surround yourself with people who know more than you. It will balance you and help you as you make decisions.

Lesson 34: Develop A Team Spirit. *Being able to work within a system is what determines greatness. Most people are able to operate effectively on their own. Yet, when put into a social setting they can crumble and are not be able to do their best. As in the game of basketball, those who make it in the game of life are the people who have mastered how to thrive in a team environment, work within a system and submit to leadership. Developing these disciplines is crucial to success.*

As team players we must understand how to contribute to, rather than take from, the team. Learning to work with others is crucial. Sometimes people are not able to work with people they've hired or reached out to for help. They just don't know how to work in groups. They have worked hard by themselves for years and are incapable of working well with others. Make an effort to master the art of working with others.

I have only gotten to where I am today because of working with others. It might be a challenge to you, but it must be a priority to understand how you fit in a team. Learn to reach out and communicate. This will help you find your place in any team. Whether you are at home, work or school, there will be times that

Instead of seeking the spotlight for ourselves, in a team your objective should be to share the spotlight and sometimes even shine the spotlight on others.[35] Basketball taught me that it takes five players to score a point. Each player has a position they must play and a territory they must cover. If a player leaves their position and tries to play someone else's position, the team will fall apart. I learned to play my position the best I could, and refused to worry about the others. My focus was on me. I had to make sure I was performing at my best to contribute all I could to the team.[36]

In my first season of basketball, the team practiced hard until our first game in October. Fortunately, I was able to hold my own on the court. I got much better at dribbling and shooting,

---

you will need to be a team player. Work hard at this, and it will really take you to new levels in whatever you do.

Lesson 35: Don't Seek the Glory for Yourself. *One of the most important rules about working on a team is putting the interest of the team ahead of your own selfish ambitions. It seems every team has someone who would rather seek the glory for themselves rather than considering everybody else. Usually that person is identified quickly and is coached on how to be a team player. Be self-aware enough to realize if this is you and change!*

Lesson 36: Stay in Your Lane. *You should always make it a point to stay in your lane and take care of yourself and your responsibilities. It is only then that you will be ready to take your place on the team and help others. Take the time to meditate on your favorite devotional or self-help book and improve yourself.*

My focus is always on my role and place on the team. The best way I can help my team and others is to first make sure I have it together. Before I try to help others, I must first know that I am leading myself well. Truthfully, ensuring I am being led by God and keeping myself on track usually takes all I have and more!

the basics of basketball, and was rewarded with a lot of playing time. Our team did very well that year, which was a big morale booster for me.[37] I felt valued as a team member.[38]

Lesson 37: Master Your Craft. *I secured a spot on my high school junior varsity basketball team because I was proficient in the basics of the sport. But, in order to excel, I had to know the ins and outs of the game far beyond the basics. Whatever your industry or career is, you must learn the rules of engagement, and master the fundamentals of your craft. That means practice, practice, practice and more practice.*

If you are playing sports, study your game plan, and put more time in it than is required. How bad do you want it? In college, go after your goals and see yourself in your job making it! In your career, don't ever see yourself in the same place a year from now. Always see yourself moving forward and gaining ground. Just as having a coach to help you with the game, you must have mentors surrounding you in the working world giving sound advice. You have the ability to set yourself up for success. Those times that no one else knows you are studying, practicing and reaching out to others will always pay off in the long run.

Lesson 38: Don't Lose Yourself. *Even on a team, you are still an individual, and you must maintain your uniqueness. Develop a sense of independence and self-value wherever you find yourself. Don't forget your personal goals and aspirations. Always remember where you are coming from and where you are going so you don't lose yourself or your way.*

For me, I keep myself accountable to have a relationship with God, my family, my employer, my pastor and then my friends. I am very strict with myself about this accountability. I don't have time to lose ground because I have lives to change. My goal is to always be ready for divine appointments that allow me to give back. You too can be ready to help others, and as you reach out to help others you will truly begin to move forward.

In the coming years, more would be required of me, but I knew that having mastered the fundamentals of the game I could only go up from there. This was a crucial lesson. You must have a solid foundation before you can build anything substantial in life.[39]

Lesson 39: Build A Solid Foundation. As we set our goals, we have to know that there is a beginning, middle and end for each goal that we've set. There is always a time of learning and training before we are ready to move into our new job or position. If we don't allow time for growth, we will lose in the end. Allow yourself time to develop in your skill.

Most of my personal success has come from having coaches throughout my life. Anytime I am around someone that I admire or have seen become successful I want to spend time with them. Gaining advice from those who are older or more experienced is so valuable. Why not benefit from those who are older and wiser? I make it a point to always listen and take notes from those who have gone ahead of me in life. If you don't have someone older and wiser who you can learn from, go and find them now!

Chapter 4

A CHAMPION IN THE SHADOWS

My first year on the team had gone great. I had a reasonable amount of playing time and had gained a lot of experience as a result. I scored lots of points during games and enjoyed the rapport of my teammates. So, as a sophomore in high school, but now on the Varsity team under Coach Harry Breland, I had high expectations of getting more playing time that year.[40]

My game was definitely at a much higher level, and so naturally I thought that it would and should translate into having lots of playing time right off. Boy! I was in for the shock of my life. I really had not given much thought to the upperclassmen that were ahead of me and how their skill might impact my place on the team.[41]

Lesson 40: You Have Earned Your Spot. *Regardless of how good you are or how you got the position, you must believe that you have earned your spot and that you bring value to the team. But most importantly, you must act like you belong where you are. When you do something great such as get on a team, land a great job or finish a hard class, you have to take time to celebrate! That experience of accomplishing something will carry you through the difficult seasons in life. Taking time to sit back and enjoy this excitement will give you the momentum you need to move on to other levels and challenges. You will find yourself saying, "If I did it then, I can do it again!"*

Lesson 41: Break Free From Entitlement Mentality. *One of the things you have to give up in a team environment is a sense of entitlement. You must value the group objectives and interests*

Each year, all the players go through a tryout that allows the coach to assess their skills, justify their inclusion on the team, as well as determine their placement. That year, the competition was stiff. The team was stacked up with a lot of seniors who had been playing together for years. These girls on the varsity team were amazing and truthfully much better, older and more experienced than I was. And so I was placed on the third string. Wow! That was so unexpected. And that meant, I would be warming up the bench quite a bit that season. I was crushed as it really felt like a huge setback. [42]

BENCH TIME IS FRUITFUL TIME

This made my second year with the team much more challenging than I had anticipated, but it was too late to back down. [43] I was neck deep in basketball; playing it, loving it and above your own. While I had earned my spot as a member of the basketball team, I had to count every opportunity to play as a privilege and not a right. I had to keep the right mindset and not assume anything. I still had to pursue wholeheartedly anything I wanted—it wouldn't just be handed to me. I wanted more playing time and would do whatever was required to get it.

Lesson 42: It's Not the End of the World. *Whether you are trying to make it on a basketball roster, a pro sports team or a new job, whenever our dreams and expectations aren't fulfilled, it can feel as though all is lost. But that is not true. It's not the end of the world. You live to fight another day. This apparent defeat could be a stepping-stone for something new. So keep your eyes open for new opportunities that will come your way.*

Lesson 43: Brace Yourself For Twists And Turns. *The way life is, you need to be firm, yet flexible at the same time. Not all of your plans and expectations will come true. And even if they do, they might happen differently, or at a different time, than you expected. So you must brace yourself emotionally and psychologically for unexpected turns. Sometimes those unexpected events are negative, other times they are positive, but you have to develop the capacity to handle both.*

determined to make something of myself in it. If I wanted to play ball then this was the way to do it. I had to be willing to flow with every aspect of it—the ups and the downs. The times I played in the game and the times I sat on the bench were all part of basketball.[44] It was hard to have my expectations for an amazing sophomore year be met with a place on the third string. But, I decided to suck it up and keep a positive attitude.[45]

All five of our starters were seniors. They really were incredible players who had paid their dues. They had all spent quite a bit of time sitting on the bench in their younger years, and their patience and effort were finally paying off with lots of playtime on the court.

_____

Lesson 44: Flow With The Game. We have to learn to adapt to change as much as possible. However, it can be harder to flow with situations when they are unfavorable. This is where you have to dig deep for inner strength. Even though I was disappointed with my position on the team, I still had to keep a good attitude.

In real life most people will quit when there is an appearance of demotion. But sometimes, if we can push through the setback, we are able to bounce back and catch a wind to the top. In the same way, when someone is fired from their job, the emotional toll and the financial stress can be enormous. But it can also be the beginning of new life and a new career. It's all about how you handle it.

Lesson 45: Keep A Positive Attitude. This is one of those things that is easier said than done. It requires you to look at your situation objectively. In order for me to excel as a player, I needed my coach and my teammates, and I could not allow my personal feelings to undermine those relationships no matter how real or legitimate those feelings were. I needed to live, act and play as though my position had stayed the same, keeping my composure and the camaraderie of my team. I could not allow any sense of frustration to set in.

The coach's desire was for this group of senior girls to go all the way and win the state championship. And they had built enough skill and experience to deliver.[46]

I, on the other hand, would definitely be playing third string, and I needed to be content with that, at least for now.[47] No one ever dreams of or anticipates starting at the bottom. But that is the way of things. In the game of life, you always start at the bottom.[48]

Lesson 46: Don't Take It Personally. It helps to see things from another perspective. The coach's priority is winning the game, and so he may not necessarily care about how anyone feels about their position or how much play time they get. His primary objective is to find players who can execute his strategy. Seen that way, it is not a matter of my lack of skill or ability but whether I fit into the coach's current strategy. Understanding that will help you deal with hurts, retain a positive self-image and keep you motivated.

Lesson 47: Taking Your Place On The Team. We all want to find and secure our spot, especially if you are playing on a team. It is healthy to have an attitude that pushes you to go for it, but be careful how you approach this. Stepping on others will not get you anywhere. At times, a team player sits back and when the time is right, they will end up climbing to a higher position and gain more playing time. Being a good sport and encouraging others when they are doing well on and off the court is a key ingredient in a great leader and a necessary ingredient to success.

Lesson 48: Starting At The Bottom. I had come from being needed on the junior varsity team as one of the key players to not being needed at all on the varsity team. Many times we must work our way up from the bottom. This might take time, but being consistent in pursuing your goal is key. Taking one day at time and working to get better each day will keep you moving forward.

When we go from one level to another we must know that each new season of our lives will bring on new challenges and experiences. For me, I needed to experience the new level of basketball that the varsity team presented. It was more fast paced

If there was one thing I needed to get used to, it was spending a lot of time on the bench. However, I was determined to get some use out of it.[49]

For the intuitive player, time on the bench is not wasted time, even though it can feel like it. There are several ways to take advantage of it and make it useful. This time can help us see where we want to go and what kind of player we want to be. On the bench, we learn what to do as well as what not to do. In addition, we see the game from a different perspective as we watch other players in action, the techniques they use and their team chemistry. From the bench, we have the time and patience to watch various moves and can see patterns and developing plays. Very simply, it gives us the opportunity to gain a coaching eye.[50]

While making the most of bench time, I also came up with

and much harder than my freshman year. I was not ready to play at this level, and I needed to understand that. Sitting back, watching, listening and learning was key to my future success.

Lesson 49: Make The Most Of The Situation! *There is a saying that that if life gives you lemons, make lemonade. I love this saying because oftentimes life will give you lemons. Learn to take advantage every opportunity, regardless of how unfavorable it may seem. Don't be quick to say no. The more you take advantage of your circumstances—positive and negative—the faster you will get to your goals.*

Lesson 50: Expand Your Vision And Skill Set. *When you watch better players and teams playing, it helps you to develop vision and a deeper understanding of the game. Also, it enables you to assimilate, internalize and develop a repertoire of playing skills and styles that will come in handy when it's your time to play.*

There is always something else to learn in your career or the industry you are in. And you can use your down times to increase your knowledge and advance your skills, making yourself even more valuable to your company or team.

a strategy to shorten my time on the bench and get me more play time. This is important because if I did nothing about it, it could take a while before I got the chance to play, if at all. There were many players on the team, and I needed to come up with a strategy to stand out from this talented crowd. My goal was to put in a lot of effort during practice and become so needed by the coach that I would eventually be promoted up to the second string. After a few weeks of executing my strategy, I had moved from third string to second string.[51] At least now I was getting more playing time.

My primary role on the second string was to be used to whip the first string players into shape and make them competitive.[52] By playing against the first string in practice,[53] I would help the entire team improve. The better defense and

---

Lesson 51: Fight Smart. *Take control of your destiny. Don't just sit down and become a victim of your circumstances. Think things through and come up with a strategy to move forward. I could have just sat there on the third string and waited for things to happen. Instead, I came up with a plan, executed it and moved up to a better place on the team.*

Lesson 52: Help Out With Someone Else's Dream. *While waiting for your dream, you may have to help with someone else's dream. Often, as you help fulfill those people's dreams, your dream is realized as well. For someone, somewhere, you are just what they need. Don't let disappointments weigh you down. Use your talents and acquired skills where they will be appreciated. Your turn will come. The more you help others to accomplish their dreams, the closer yours will be.*

Lesson 53: Know Your Team. *Know the strongest and weakest players on the team. Learn from the strongest and the best, and help the weakest and the average to get better. This will help make you indispensable. Always look for ways to benefit a team. We all have talents that can help a team. We just have to look for where we fit best for the good of the team.*

offense I played, the better the team would get.[54] I loved playing defense. My talent was to steal balls from the other team. I probably aggravated the first string as I would sometimes go after them pretty hard. But, I didn't know any better way to get them prepared to beat the opposing teams.[55]

Practices were great when we are all playing one another. I always hoped that at the end of each practice the coach would notice my efforts—that a play I made would catch his attention, and maybe he would give me more playing time. I played so hard just to hear my name called out when I did something worth making a fuss over. I would work even harder when I got the coach's encouragement, leaving practice sure that I would get to play in the next game. But I never did.[56]

Being on the bench was tough. I desperately wanted to be one of the five players in the heat of the action. In this season, I learned to support my teammates whether I was playing or not.

_____

Lesson 54: Know Your Role On The Team. I wasn't ready for a lot of game playing time yet, but I had an important role to play— helping my teammates become better prepared. Often we are put in a place that is not comfortable. When that happens, we have to make the most of it, and take our place. In due time we will get that promotion!

Lesson 55: Give Your Best To The Team. You may not be the best player on the team, but you can give your best to the team. Regardless of how insignificant you think your role is, make sure to always do your best. It counts!

Lesson 56: Always Stay Hopeful. It can be hard to stay optimistic when you keep going through cycles of defeat and disappointments. But, you have to be strong and stay hopeful in the midst of chronic difficulties. Believe that there are better days ahead for you. To be successful you must have a positive outlook on life, regardless of your circumstances.

Instead of thinking about me and how great I could play if only I had a chance, I had to stop and accept the time on the bench. My time to shine would come.[57]

While on the bench, I still had to keep my head up and enjoy the game.[58] I would cheer for my team and help the other players when I could.[59] I did my best to keep focused on my ultimate goal. Every day, as I went into practice, I set my mind to play at the top of my game.

Lesson 57: Not Every Moment Is Yours. You need to be relentless as you pursue your dreams. However, sometimes no matter how hard you try or how much skill or experience you have, things can just stay the same. The stagnation often has nothing to do with your skill level or efforts and everything to do with your season.
Not every moment is yours, and you have to realize when your opportune moment has not yet come. Be patient and keep preparing so that when your time to shine comes, and it surely will, you will have all the resources and tools to excel. My time on the bench was needed to learn things I would need in the future.

Lesson 58: Actively Wait Your Turn. The biggest challenge in life is watching everyone else seem to move forward while things continue to stay the same for you. You must learn to be active while waiting for your turn. There is a lot you can do to make yourself more marketable; go to school, practice piano, exercise, learn a second language, etc. In real life, there are reasons why you may still be on the bench. Find out what is causing the delay and whatever it is continue to work hard at improving yourself while you wait.

Lesson 59: Celebrate The Seasons And Victories Of Others. When others are in their season, shining in the spotlight while you are still on the bench, it can be hard to cheer for them. But learn to cheer for and celebrate the wins of those currently in the spotlight. That's the only way to keep team spirit alive and for you to stay motivated.

Though there was not a starter position for me on the team, I was determined to become the best relief player for anyone of the starters.[60] This way, I could become the go-to-girl for the coach. If a player is having a bad day and the coach needed someone who is ready to go at a moment's notice and make things happen, I wanted to be the coach's first thought. It was important that he knew that he could count on me. When all else failed and the coach's options were limited, he would think of Chantell.

And then, one day during a game, it paid off. Coach Breland called my name,[61] "Mayes!" After all those practices, I could finally show him that I had what it took to contribute to the team during game time.[62] That day, I played great defense and stole a couple of balls. I probably made the offense a little

Lesson 60: Don't Be Paralyzed By Stagnation. When others appear to be succeeding and you feel stuck, make sure it doesn't discourage you to the point where you feel paralyzed. Keep your focus on your objectives, and remember that your time to shine will come. Don't let yourself be consumed with jealousy, envy or disappointment. They will undermine your drive to succeed and ultimately drag you down. Just give 100 percent each day. Learn to do this when times are down and when times are up. When you can give of yourself fully even when you don't feel like it, that is the sign of a great leader.

Lesson 61 : Be Ready To Jump In. The opportunity you are looking for may come at a moment's notice and you have to be ready to seize it. This is why you can't allow yourself to be distracted or discouraged. You don't want to be caught off guard or unprepared and ruin the opportunity of a lifetime. I was not expecting to be called into the game, but thankfully I was always prepared. So when the coach called, I was able to deliver.

Lesson 62: Life Is An Ongoing Audition. You must see every opportunity as your audition for the next big act. Every moment has the potential to change your life forever. I always say, "Be On Ready at all times." You never know when your time will come.

mad because I was so ready for some playing time.[63] It makes me laugh now to think back on how I felt that day. Just that little bit of time on the court fueled me for at least another month on the bench! I had caught the vision. I could almost reach out and feel victory.

So during the rest of the year, I would come on and off the bench, getting short times to play. The coach was getting me ready to play in future years as my skill improved. I needed that experience of getting out there on the court, to get a feel of the ball and see how I would react in intense moments of pressure. The coach would not risk keeping me in the game too long.[64] But just the short times I played gave me the experience I needed. It was all about the delicate act of balancing exposure with preparation. I needed to experience the feel of a real game in order to be ready. However, it had to be at the least possible cost to the team and the game currently underway.[65]

Lesson 63: Don't Hold Back. When the moment comes, don't hold back. Whenever you have an opportunity to demonstrate your talent, go all the way. You may never have a second chance. Make every moment count. Keep your confidence high, believe you can and you will!

Lesson 64: There's A Winning Strategy. There is a place for playing sports for fun, but we were playing to win and that required a strategy. Sometimes a winning strategy means that you play a little less prominent role or that you are a little more hands-off than usual. Find your winning strategy and work it.

Lesson 65: Coach Knows Best. It doesn't matter how intelligent, skilled or innovative you are; it's important to realize that others have gone ahead of you. There's always somebody who is capable of making you better and helping you excel in your field. If I was going to reach my potential as a basketball player, I needed to lean on the instruction of the coach.

PLAYING TO WIN

One time, the coach called me into the game when one of the starters was racking up too many fouls.[66] I knew this was my opportunity to shine. Basketball is not just about being athletic, but also about being strategic in your movements and passes. As soon as I got in the game, I began looking for an open spot on the court to bounce-pass the ball or to run through for a layup shot.

A few minutes into play, I saw my opportunity.[67] My opponents were messy with their dribbling, and in a bold move I stole the ball from one of them.[68] I was so nervous. With my heart beating out of my chest, I dribbled towards the basket, weaving in-and-out of the other players.[69]

Lesson 66: Be In The Moment. Prepare yourself for the day you get called out. It might be a promotion, a chance to make your mark on the playing field, or a once in a lifetime opportunity. Whatever it is, make sure you are ready for your big day.

Lesson 67: Be Strategic In Your Actions. Be strategic in your approach to life. Whether at school, in a job or, yes, even picking a church that you want to join, you have to be strategic. You must think things through, weigh the pros and cons, and then make a move. Always stay a few steps ahead so you won't be caught off guard. Knowing and understanding who you are will give you confidence to be strategic in your future.

Lesson 68: Go And Take It. There are times that you don't wait for the moment; you get out there and take it. The coach had already given me the opportunity, the rest was up to me. This was my chance to show the coach I could be of value when I was needed. When the door opens for something new, I jump at the opportunity. Don't be among the average who don't make any moves. Live above average, taking action with your life.

Lesson 69: Learn To Maneuver Through. In order to overcome obstacles you may need to recruit special help. Other times you may need retraining. Every obstacle you overcome gets you closer and closer to your objective.

Just as I was about to shoot the ball, a player on the other team pushed me.[70] This is a classic move. Sometimes it's an accident, but usually it's intentional and comes from playing poor defense.[71] As a result, the referee called a foul on my opponent.[72]

Realizing what I needed to do, I walked to the foul line, prepared to make two shots and tie up our game. The team was fired up and gave me pats on the back, offering encouraging words. I knew I had to make the shots. This was my chance to showcase all my hard work. I had trained so hard for this one opportunity. It was do or die in my mind.[73]

Lesson 70: Beware Of Malicious Attacks. There are obstacles to overcome, but often the hurdles we face in life are not systems or finances, but people. Someone may deliberately sabotage you or your efforts. People who have a very positive outlook on life or a great sense of optimism tend not to factor this into their dealings with others. Beware!

Lesson 71: Maintain Your Composure. Regardless of how desperate you are or how fast your competitors may seem to be gaining ground, don't let your emotions and insecurities get the better of you, or you may do something you regret. Stay calm, maintain your composure and execute your counter strategies.

Lesson 72: Pay Attention To The Rules. As you push for success in your life, career or business, always consider the ethics and legalities. Make sure the pressures of life do not push you to be reckless and disregard the rules. That can come back to haunt you.

Lesson 73: The Stakes Are Always High. That day, the team depended on me to pull it through. I had to carry the weight of the position I played and would not allow the other team to score on my playing time. I had to be on-point with my game. There was no room for failure.

You must make the shot! When your time comes, and the door opens for you to step up, make sure you have put in the effort needed to be successful. There will be times in your life when you

At a moment like this, there are so many things going through your mind—bend your knees, check your hand placement and guide the ball to basket. I had to remember everything I had learned the last two years.[74] There was so much pressure,[75] but I knew that this was the moment that I had been preparing for.[76] I had sat on the bench during games, but I was working my tail off in practice to make sure that if I played for even a few seconds in a game, I would make them count.[77]

---

won't have enough time to think your decisions through before you must execute. All that hard work you did in the past will pay off in those moments.

Lesson 74: Execute With Knowledge. *All the lessons you learn count—the time on the bench, that little tip from a teammate, a rebuke from the coach. Both the pleasant and the unpleasant ones count in those crucial, game-changing moments. When your moment comes, be ready to make it happen using the valuable insight gained from those around you.*

Lesson 75: Loosen Up. *Don't let the stress get to you. Not every opportunity in life will have hundreds or thousands of fans watching. But it can sure feel like it when the stakes are high. Psych yourself up, loosen up and don't let the pressure get to you. Being stressed out will hurt your performance.*

Lesson 76: Be Confident In Your Abilities. *Of all the people in the world, you are in that spot at that particular time in history because you are capable. You deserve to be there. So remember that, and be confident in your moment. Often, all the years of preparation are leading up to just one defining moment.*

Lesson 77: Every Practice Is Game Time. *It was always game on for me. I took the practices just as seriously as the game itself. With that as my motto, I was always ready. If you take every opportunity to practice your skills as though it were an opportunity of a lifetime, when that lifetime opportunity comes you won't have to worry about how to perform. You will excel.*

I looked up at the basketball hoop one last time. I took a deep breath and made the first shot. I heard cheers around me, but it felt like my life was in slow motion as I bounced the ball on the line, concentrating on what I had to do. I made the second shot, and a sense of relief passed over me.[78] It was a moment of victory, not only for me personally but also for the team. I was ecstatic. I had just made two shots in a very competitive and important game. But there would be time to celebrate and take it all in later.[79]

After I made the shots, the coach quickly pulled me out of the game and replaced me with a starter. I knew that was going to happen when I went in; however, I chose not to let it bother me.[80] Otherwise, it could have affected my ability to concentrate and make the shots. I made sure to show my worth on the court however short the moment was.

Looking back at my time on the bench, I realize that it holds a great lesson about climbing up the ladder of success. We all have something to prove, but our success depends on timing. Sometimes you just have to wait your turn. I advise young entrepreneurs to hang in there because their day will come.

Lesson 78: Get Your Priorities Straight. *Being cheered on was good, but making the basket was better. When your moment comes, get your priorities straight. Even good things can become distractions and cost you the opportunity for success if you let them.*

Lesson 79: Your Impact Is Universal. *Always remember that a lot of people are counting on your success in life. Your victory is for many, some of whom you may never meet in this life. It matters that you succeed. So don't give up—for you and for those you will impact.*

Lesson 80: Don't Get Distracted By Worry. *It's easy to move too many steps ahead of ourselves and not take full advantage of, or even enjoy, the current moment. Whether my coach would use me in future games was something to be concerned about later. Right now, I was needed, and I executed. I stayed in the moment.*

There is always a process to get you to where you want to be. Hard work and training have to take place. You can't jump from point 'A' to point 'C' without first going through 'B' to get to 'C.' If you skip a step, you risk losing foundational pieces you will need for future success. Bench time is crucial for your success. It is a must in life. Even though difficult, that is how you get yourself ready for that big day of promotion.[81]

WE WON

That year, my sophomore year and only the second year I had played basketball, our team went to the state finals, and we won. Wow! It felt really great to be on the winning side. I may not have played in any of the championship games leading up to the finals, but with every tackle and bruise in practice, every tear and cheer from the bench, I helped my teammates prepare for this victory.[82] My name is proudly listed on a banner

---

Lesson 81: Your Time Will Come. There is always a tendency to wonder if success will ever happen to you, especially when you have been through a long hard season of failure and drought. But, there is a time and season for everything, and you must believe that your time to shine will come. Repeat that to yourself as often as you remember, and it will help you stay motivated in the tough times. All the days of waiting and preparation will pay off, and you will have your day in the sun.

The question is what to do with yourself in the down times. Because it does matter what you do with the days on the bench— those long periods of waiting. Those are the toughest years, but you must put them to good use. They help you learn how to fall and rise up, how to feel defeat and bounce back, and how to keep your head up when the tide is against you. What you do with those years in the shadows will define who you will become when you are finally in the spotlight.

Lesson 82: You Are Indispensable. The term MVP, Most Valuable Player, is given to specific individuals for exceptional performance in a game or an amazing contribution to a win. Soldiers are awarded special medals in recognition of their valor or acts of courage in battle.

in the school gym along with those incredible players. I was so honored that day to just sit with the winning team.

If you had told me that not even two years after I had taken on basketball, I would become a Champion, I would have laughed in your face. To be a Champion is just an item on a wish list for most people, and it was for me too. But it actually happened to me, and it was because of the team I played on. What was once an impossible dream became a reality in my very young career as a high school basketball player in a little town in Mississippi. No matter where you are or what stage of career you are in, you too can become a winner. Very important questions to ask are, what team are you playing on, and who is coaching you?

But a stay-at-home mom may never receive any public recognition for what she does.

Whether you are recognized publicly or privately for your contributions to your team, or never recognized at all, it is important to remember that you are an MVP. Without you the team would not be the same. We all have a position to play in order to help our team win. It might not always be in the spotlight, and you may be hidden sometimes. But while you are hidden, shine even there. It will pay off later.

Chapter 5

THE LIFE OF A CHAMPION

The life of a champion does not begin when you make your first million dollars, or when all of your dreams have come true, and you live in a nice house, fly first class or stay in the nicest hotels. No, it begins much earlier, long before you hold a trophy in your hands, earn any accolades or rewards. You become a champion when you start believing, thinking and acting like one.[83]

I had already won a championship as a sophomore, but that was just the beginning. I needed to think and live like one. My junior year was a trial by fire that, even though difficult, moved me further down the road to being the Champion I knew I was.

MORE LEARNING

In my junior year, I had finally reached the level of starter. We still had Harry Breland as our head coach. All the seniors from the year before, our championship year, had moved on to life after high school. Finally there was room at the top. This was my season to shine; new role, new team. Unfortunately, I didn't realize the impact all these new changes would have on the team, so I approached practice and games as though everyone already knew me, confident in my basketball skills and my place on the team.

Lesson 83: See Yourself Winning. It matters what you believe, how you think and the way you see yourself. I have always believed that I can conquer whatever I set my sights on. So, whether at a practice or a game, before I set foot on the basketball court, I made sure my mind was right, and I was ready to win.

This was a devastating mistake. Consequently, I learned a lesson about the social aspect of the game.[84]

THE SOCIAL GAME

To succeed at basketball or any game for that matter, you need to have talent as well as skill. However, these are not the only factors that determine success. If you want to excel, you have to take the social dimension of the game into consideration.

Sadly, there are many talented and skilled players who have not developed the social skills necessary to go above and beyond in their career. There are players who could have made it all the way to the professional level, been very successful and even famous, but the lack of basic interpersonal skills stopped them from progressing any further from where they were. I realized very early on that even at the high school level, if I was going to be successful, I would have to play a different kind of game, one with a greater degree of social awareness.[85]

I want to clarify as well emphasize that having great social skills does not merely mean that you able to strike up

----

Lesson 84: Be Aware When Change Is Occurring. *It may seem like change should be obvious. But it can be painfully easy to overlook. A different co-worker joins your team and before you realize it, the entire dynamic of the team has shifted. Make sure you pay attention to the changes occurring around you. Is the culture of your workplace changing? Adapt to it. Is your teacher expecting more from you than you expected? Meet her expectations. Don't assume that just because you haven't changed, your environment hasn't changed. The consequences could be dire.*

Lesson 85: Look Around You. *Having excellent social skills is not optional if you want to win. Be aware of your social surroundings and the interactions, transactions and politics that take place around you both on and off the court. Are you invited to parties? Do people trust you with secrets? Do you have to fight for the ball? These are all clues as to your current social status that can help you determine if you need to up your social game.*

conversations and relate to others successfully. No, there is more to it. It is also about being able to navigate complex social environments and harness relationships to fulfill your objectives. It is like dribbling a ball, except in this case the ball represents human interaction and connections, and the goal is some personal or group advantage.[86] Having great social skills usually requires a little bit more thought and effort on our part. It is something that must be learned.

The first rule in winning the social game is to have a good relationship with the people in authority. If there is one person who wields a lot of power and influence in basketball, it is the coach. He is the primary decision maker on the court and reserves the right to decide who plays and who sits out on the bench.[87] So it is to your advantage to have great rapport with the coach. I needed to include in my strategy a plan to win the coach and stay in his good books.

_____

Lesson 86: Learn The Social Game. Beyond the court, there is another game with stakes equally as high as that played on the court. It is the social game. No one teaches you how to play, the scoreboard is invisible, and yet winners and losers are regularly declared. This game has a serious impact on what happens on the court. You must learn to play and win this game if you want to succeed in life.

Lesson 87: Get To Know The Gatekeepers. In the game of basketball, building rapport with your coach is very important. Moreover, in the high school setting there are others who always carry a lot of influence, sometimes to the point of fighting with the coach for control. These are the gatekeepers of the game.

In order to win the social game, you must get to know the gatekeepers—the people who make things happen. Begin to explore how to connect with them in a meaningful or advantageous way. No matter your industry or career, you must get to know the major players in your own social game.

In order to accomplish that, I decided to be intentional on the court and align myself with the coach's vision of the game.[88] I knew the coach would appreciate a person who was striving to be the kind of player he wanted. Also, I decided that whether the coach's decision or attitudes toward me were favorable or not, I would continue to give him the respect he deserved and would not second guess his decisions regarding the team.[89] It doesn't matter how talented you are, if you are insubordinate no one will want to work with you, because you will ruin the team spirit wherever you go.

LOCKER ROOM EXPERIENCE

Next to winning the coach is winning your teammates. This is perhaps more challenging than you would think. On a high school girls' basketball team, it's next to impossible. It is definitely much easier to win the coach. All you have to do is just play his game, right? What if that won't cut it? How do you try to please a group of high school teenage girls? For one, stay away from their boyfriends! But is that enough? Definitely not, and I learned that in a very painful way.

Lesson 88: Win The Coach. The first rule of winning is to win the coach. You have to play the coach's game, not your game. Learn to do things the way your supervisors want. There is a certain level of dedication and professionalism that wins you the admiration of your supervisors. Strive for this, and you will be well on your way to winning the social game.

Lesson 89: Submit To The Coach. In sports, the coach is the first member of the team. However, in real life the coach is not always seen as part of the team, and so they are not always included in crucial decision making. There would be a lot more wins in life if coaches and mentors had as much power as they do in a game of basketball or any other game.

So, you have to make the choice to find a coach or mentor and to submit to him or her. Most corporations have board members experienced in their fields who help make very important decisions. Find your 'board members' and trust their judgment.

One of the most hurtful experiences of my life happened after a basketball practice in my junior year. I had noticed some strange behavior during the practice;[90] my teammates would not throw the ball to me. I would be wide open for the ball, and they would deliberately throw the ball to someone else who had two people guarding them. After a couple of days of this horrible feeling of being exiled by the team, I went to Coach Breland and asked him what I was doing wrong. He said that he had noticed it too and would deal with it. I had no idea how he planned to resolve it or that by the end of that day he would actually do something about it. [91]

So, that same day after practice, the coach told us all to go to the locker room, because he wanted to talk with us. Once all the team was gathered, he said, "Some of you girls who have issues with Chantell need to get it out, and we need to get to the bottom of this." I was in shock—it was completely unexpected.

Lesson 90: Win The Team. *You have to be a little more tactful in the way you handle yourself and others if you want to win the team. Diplomacy is probably too much to expect of a high school student, but I had to rise to the occasion. I learned that getting along with my teammates was as important as the way I relate to my coach. The two go hand-in-hand. So, I made a point to prioritize the horizontal relationships with fellow teammates while building and maintaining that vertical relationship with the coach.*

Lesson 91: Tread Carefully. *When you find yourself in a group, don't let the pressure to fit in get to you. If it does, it can cause you to say and do things that could ruin someone's reputation or yours. My teammates were obviously upset at me, and had discussed me behind my back, causing a confusing and extremely hurtful situation.*

Whatever you do, stay away from conversations or connections that will sow seeds of discontent with the team or disrespect for the coach. If these seeds take root in your mind, they are bound to reflect in your relationships and performance. These things can get bad to the point that you may have to leave the team.

My heart dropped. I didn't like confrontation. All I wanted was just to be a part of the team.[92] But it was too late; the cat was already out of the bag.

The complaints of my teammates varied from my playing style to my facial expressions.[93] Some of the girls mentioned that they did not like how I played. I was a rather strong defensive player, perhaps a little too aggressive, and so I had rubbed some of the girls the wrong way. Remember that my main talents were my speed and that I could play defense very well. So it was a rather shocking discovery that my team considered my strong

---

Lesson 92: Face Conflict Head On. *Most of the time we want to hide our head in the sand, like an ostrich, and wish that conflict would resolve itself. If you find yourself dealing with conflict within a group, make sure to do everything to resolve it promptly. If not, it can ruin the team spirit, reduce the team's performance and eventually, it could actually lead to someone being removed from the team.*

What if one person had come to me and shared the concerns of the team, rather than them all treating me as the enemy? This situation could have been resolved more quickly and much less traumatically. There is a real danger to a team's effectiveness when issues are blown up rather than dealt with quickly and decisively.

You are a better person when you are able to face opposition and deal with conflict. I always say, "Take the high road." It is less stressful! If you try, you can always find something useful to learn out of any situation, no matter how difficult. Remember that facing conflict head on does not mean you should not be tactful or considerate. It's not a license to be rude!

Lesson 93: Be Aware Of Individual Differences, Values, Preferences. *Everyone has their preferences and values. What someone calls petty may actually be a very big deal to someone else. It may not always be rational, but if a teammate or coworker feels that something is important to them make sure to treat it that way. Other people's perceptions may not be wrong...they might just be different.*

defensive playing a major flaw. However, that was the least traumatizing part of the exchange.

FACIAL EXPRESSIONS COUNT

No, the hardest part of this team meeting was when they shared their impressions of my facial expressions and described how they didn't like them. The thing is, I was a very emotional player, probably too emotional. I always wanted to take it to the next level. I was a hard working player, and I was determined to go to the top so when I missed a shot or didn't run a play right you could see it all over my face. That is what the girls were referring to, and it hurt.

As I sat there being lectured to, I knew I had to dig deep for the strength to get through this.[94] I hoped that at any moment the coach would step in and defend me, but that did not happen.[95] I think he was using this to teach me how to rise up and handle difficult situations. It was the hardest thing I have ever gone through, but it's probably the best lesson I have ever learned. I was so embarrassed. I told the girls I was sorry for my actions. I truly didn't know what else to do.

I drove home in tears that day. Many questions and thoughts flooded my mind. How was I supposed to go back there, look them in the face and play ball with them? But I had to. This was my team.

Lesson 94: Develop Your Emotional Capacity. The people who hurt you the most are often those you need the most. No matter how much you feel hurt, rejected or mistreated, you must learn how to dig deep and harness hidden resources and depths to cope. That way you won't lose relationships or collaborators that are crucial to your success in life.

Lesson 95: Learn To Isolate And Contain Conflict. The coach did not have any issues with me, and he avoided being caught in the middle of the controversy. Sometimes, when we have problems with one member of a group we transfer the sentiments to others who are not connected at all and ruin everyone's spirits. Take my coach's example, and avoid this pitfall.

I knew I couldn't hold on to the pain and let it kill my desire to be part of this team.[96] The only way I could get back to playing on the team with good spirits was to forgive and move on.[97]

YOU CAN FACE THE DAY

The next day, I went to practice, and I just kept going as though nothing had happened. To be sure, I took some of their criticism to heart and changed as best I could. The other stuff, I just had to let go.[98] I learned the importance of people's perceptions of me. I tried not to let everyone see me in a negative light as I played on the court—I became more self-aware, and watched my facial expressions from that day forward.

Lesson 96: You Must Get Along. A house divided cannot stand. Even if the individual members of a team are very skilled, if they don't learn to get along and work together they cannot be successful. So when you are choosing a team, or one to become part of, consider how well they work together. Can you get along with each person? If not, why not? And if they are important for the performance of the team, how can you make things work?

Lesson 97: Don't Hold Grudges—Get Over It And Move On. Even on a team that is very united, offenses will happen as time goes on. If things don't come out in the open, the hurt can eat at you and create emotional distance. Even if the issues do come out, you must learn to forgive, completely forget, get over it and move on.

Lesson 98: Self Examine—Look In The Mirror. The people in our lives are supposed to help make us better. They don't always do it in the right or nicest way, but there may be some nugget of truth in their criticism. So don't be quick to shut them down or close your ears to them.

After the initial denial, disbelief and highly charged emotions that come with confrontation, take a moment to examine yourself to see if there is room for improvement. I knew I had to take the team's criticism with a good attitude. In these situations, take what you feel is helpful and throw out the rest.

I also learned to be selective with how I showed my emotions during games. As an athlete, I was in the spotlight. Therefore, I needed to be careful about what a fan might observe. I did not need everyone knowing how I felt when I messed up out on the court.[99] You see, I may have been winning the game on the court, but there was another game, in the locker room, that I was losing big time because I was not even aware that it existed.[100]

Lesson 99: Control Your Emotions. *If we give full expression to negative emotions such as anger, the result can be disastrous. In the same way, positive emotions such as joy can energize us to achieve great things. Learn how to direct your emotional energies. Both positive and negative emotions can be seen as excessive or inappropriate depending on the forum. So whether in public or in private, don't let your emotions control you. Watch what you say and do at all times.*

Lesson 100: Develop Your Social Skills. *I had to learn the rules of winning, and that meant knowing the ins and the outs of the game beyond the technical sphere, beyond the court, and into the locker room, the hallways, the cafeteria and yes, even the classrooms.*

You must learn the rules of engagement. For someone, that might mean learning to play golf. For another it requires learning to play pool. Learn to engage beyond the immediate work environment. That's how you expand your social circle. Those connections can then lead to other deeper connections.

Start by improving your current relationships. You have to invest time, energy, goodwill and kindness into the people in your life now. When you strengthen your relationship with one person, he will naturally introduce you to his circle of friends, and as you continue to put value on those relationships and invest in them, your circle expands.

THE GAME CHANGE

There needed to be a paradigm shift in my approach to the game, both on and off the court. Being a tough defensive player was not enough. I needed to factor in the fan zone and the locker room, where friendships are made and the ball is passed even before we hit the court.[101] I had to break out of my comfort zone, out of my little world, and develop relationships within the team that I otherwise would not have.[102]

Lesson 101: Be Friendly. Whether on or off the court, you cannot take emotions and personal feelings out of human interactions. The fact is, it is easier to pass the ball to a teammate who is friendly than to one who is rude or not so nice. You must place value on each team member and endeavor to have great working relationships with them. The key to your success in life may lie with that one teammate you don't like much or that you don't like to talk to at all.

Lesson 102: Challenge Your Prejudices. I was in a situation where I had no option but to force myself to change. Most people don't feel like they have to make any adjustments in the way they relate to others. And some people can go their entire lives without any meaningful interaction with someone outside of their immediate circle.

However, if you seek to be successful you have to face your weaknesses. There is a great relationship, possibly a lifelong friendship, on the other side of your biases, pride and prejudices. You have to determine to challenge yourself and reach out to others in order to gain the benefits of these unexplored relationships.

I had to come to maturity as a person—a fully functional social being.[103] As part of that journey, I made it a point not to isolate anyone. I had been the subject of gossip and had been ridiculed. I knew the impact that it had on me. So, I decided to not exclude or malign others. This can be a fine line to walk as you risk being isolated yourself. However, I flow better in an atmosphere of collaboration. While it was a tough call, I made it anyway.[104]

The experience that day in the locker room changed my life forever. I look back now, and I certainly appreciate the opportunity I had for correction. It didn't feel very good then, but I took it and ran with it. I made the changes that were within my power to make in my bid to develop a better rapport with my teammates.

Lesson 103: Take The Higher Road. Always learn from others; even their criticism can be valuable. We all want to be great at what we do. Many times we have to learn through trials and challenges what needs to be changed in our lives in order to become great.

That difficult day in the locker room has helped me throughout the years. Even though not everything said about me was accurate, I didn't fight back. I learned that being a team player sometimes required personal change and sacrifice. I now refer back to that day in the locker room as I build teams in the corporate world. Even though it was difficult I learned everything I could from it and was determined to win this social game.

Lesson 104: Don't Isolate Anyone. In every social setting, certain people connect more easily than others regardless of gender, ethnicity or other factors. You will naturally have an easy connection or flow with certain teammates that you may not necessarily have with others. However, it is important to put value on all teammates.

Make every effort to develop rapport with each member of the team. I learned to never isolate someone—more damage can be done than anyone could ever imagine. Always reach out to others and take it as a learning experience; what areas should you change so you are able to get along better with others?

Chapter 6

ALWAYS A CHAMPION

Time has a way of sneaking up on you. Before you know it, it is here. The tide of time tends to thrust you forward into the future and the unknown, prepared or otherwise. It does not give you much room or choice. Neither does it seek your counsel or cooperation. Ready or not, I was now a senior in high school, and there were expectations, from parents, teachers, coaches and teammates.

READY TO PLAY BALL

As a senior I was considered one of the experienced players on the team,[105] and with that, the pressures mounted.

Lesson 105: Create Your Identity And Build A Reputation. While on the bench, I had carved out an identity as the most aggressive defensive player on the second string. That eventually opened the door for me to become a starter. This is where you must take the social dimension of the game seriously. It's not just about the skill you possess, but how others perceive your attitude and approach to the game.

No matter how small, once you have identified a need and are filling it, create a reputation of success. This is a way to further stand out. Don't get caught up in looking for something big when what you need is right in front of you.

There has to be a starting place, so take whatever comes your way, whether it is a job opportunity or a position on a team, and make the best of it. Be proud of yourself and where you are. I always say, "Blow it out of the water wherever you are placed." Over time you will rise up, and the vast and invaluable experience you have acquired will guide you down the road.

But there was also a buildup of excitement. It seemed that I had been waiting for this moment all my life. In my first year, I played on the junior varsity team and enjoyed a good amount of playing time, developing my confidence. I spent my second year with the team on the bench playing mostly second string as I helped my teammates and improved my game. In my third year, I was finally a starter, and I learned a lot about interpersonal relationships. And now, here I was, in my fourth year, now a senior. I had matured as a player and all my experiences were coming together. I was looking forward to starting and actually enjoying it!

But there were other changes that had occurred over the summer. We had a new coach, Wayne Folkes. By this time, I knew the impact of change, and it brought the question of where I would fit into the team. Would Coach Folkes see my ability?[106]

When the roster was posted that season, I had made it to first string. Hallelujah! It was not entirely unexpected, but it was still a great relief, and I celebrated. My time to shine had come, finally! All the experiences on the bench, in the shadows and being

---

Lesson 106: Do Not Be Defined Or Confined. *I could not control the coach's perception of my skills or readiness, neither could I determine who he would choose to start. But I could control my perception of myself and the choices I made. I chose to believe that I was as qualified as anyone of the starters. As I saw myself that way both on and off the court, I began to position myself and play that way.*

This is very important. Whatever your dream or vision is, don't let setbacks or complications cause you to look down on yourself or your abilities. Don't ever believe the competition is better than you. If you believe in yourself, success is within reach. Anytime I start a new position at work or have a new opportunity, I always take time to step back and take a survey of the team assembled. This could take a few weeks of figuring out how I fit in and where my talents can be used. Once I feel confident of my role in this new team I move forward secure in the knowledge that no one else can fill my position on this team.

misunderstood had led up to this one point. It was time to put my skills to use in primetime. But more than that, it was a calling into leadership. I needed to take my place as a leader, and be a role model for younger players.

For most of us when we dream of being in the limelight we think only of the pleasures and not the pressures. We tend to focus on the positive aspects and block out the undesirable parts. However, there are stresses and challenges that come with promotion as well as being in leadership, and you must be ready for them. When my time came to play first string, I was grateful for that year on the bench, because it prepared me for the role. I had the athletic skills to perform at that level, as well as the emotional and social intelligence required. I had matured enough for the whole package.

KNOW THYSELF

At this point, I knew what I was good at. I was a player with a couple of talents. I could run very fast and play very strong defense.[107] Also, strategically I had improved a lot as a player. I had mastered my game and would visualize myself on the court stealing balls. I got to where I could read the play before it happened. I would watch facial expressions and movements and could pretty much gauge where the ball was going. If you put enough pressure on the person with the ball, at some point there will be a turnover. That year I won best defensive player, and was so proud of myself.[108]

Lesson 107: Be Secure In Your Abilities and Limitations. In order to excel in life you have to come to a place of maturity regarding your abilities and your limitations. You should have pride in what you know and what you can do but not be ashamed at what you don't know and what you can't do.

Lesson 108: Become A Specialist. Identify a need and fill it. When the competition gets stiff, and it always does, it's important to find unique ways to stand out. In order to make yourself valuable and indispensable, you have to search out and identify needs in your career or industry, and become very good at meeting those needs. Become so valuable that when you are not around everyone misses your contribution. That is a niche you have filled.

With all my excellence and improvement in defense, there were areas of skill and performance that I was certain I should leave alone and not waste my time and energy on. The fact is I was not an all-around player.

I was not very good at shooting and scoring. I wanted so badly to be a great shooter, but I just wasn't. I was a pretty determined girl, and I put a lot of time, effort and practice into it in the early years of basketball. But it just didn't click.[109]

In my sophomore year, I didn't set out to be a relief player. However, the nature of the game makes it necessary to replace players every now and then. It may be due to injury or because a player may be out of sorts on that particular day. The coach can either just pick someone at random to meet those needs or I can position myself in such a way that I become that "random choice," because the coach knows that I will deliver. Whatever role you choose, be the best. I knew offense wasn't my role, but I owned the defense!

Lesson 109: Take Control—Focus On What's Within Reach.
Basketball doesn't give you a lot of time to waste. I didn't have the luxury of waiting around to see if I would become a great offensive player. I had to go after what I was good at—defense! Unfortunately in life, many people spend too much time worrying and complaining about what they don't have, wasting and under-utilizing their talents instead of rising up and pushing for what they can get. Don't settle for second best, but make sure you don't despise a golden opportunity that may look different than you expected.

We usually don't want to go through the process to get to our destination. But gaining the experience offered by different opportunities can help make you a success. In my journey to success, I took every opportunity to learn many different jobs within my company. Those days were the days that made me who I am today. I never thought I was too good for any of those jobs. Remember that there is always a reason you go through those hard times. We can't see the end result, but I guarantee you it will pay off somewhere down the road.

What happened is that I was so fast in going after balls and playing defense that by the time I got down the court I couldn't slow myself down mentally to make a fluid shot. Even free throws were a challenge. Because of my defensive skills, I would rack up so many fouls for my team, you would not believe it. But converting them into points was rather difficult. If I could have made all those foul shots I would have averaged at least 15-20 points per game just on free throw shots alone. I laugh at it today!

TEAM CHEMISTRY

Once I realized my strengths I learned to focus on what I was good at and utilize my team for what I was not good at.[110] Yes, it is important to develop your weaknesses, but when it is game time you don't have the luxury for trial and error. You must learn to let others make up for those weaknesses. So, my team became an extension of me. I began to rely on my team to make the shots I could not make.[111]

I played hard, stole balls and gave them to my teammates. They knew when I was going after the ball to be ready for me to steal it or for it to go out of bounds and create a turnover. They were always ready for the pass or another opportunity to throw the ball in from the out-of-bounds line. It felt good to know that I was good at something and could contribute. I loved passing the ball and then assisting on a shot. I did not have to push myself to try and make every shot. That's what my team was for.

***

Lesson 110: Zone In On Your Strengths. In life, when you discover what you are good at, you have to zone in on it. Invest time and energy in what you are passionate about and what you are good at. Trying to balance many things at once can wear you down, and you won't excel in that one thing you are really good at, because you have your focus on too many things.

Lesson 111: Resist The Pressure of the Glory. When there are hundreds of fans watching, there is the temptation to want to be spectacular and get fans to cheer. But getting cheers is not the objective, winning is! That requires excellent teamwork. Let your team be an extension of you and help make the shots you can't make yourself.

In teamwork, we all have to find that sweet spot where we do what we are best at and leave the rest to others. We need to be good at playing our part and even better at passing to others. If you have the right team that understands the "pass off," then you are definitely going to be successful. The "pass off" is the most difficult thing to understand and execute on a team. People usually hold on to the ball longer than they should, and sometimes inexperienced and anxious players can "pass off" too soon.

Striking the right balance is the key to success on a team. Individual players must play their best and release the ball at a strategic time to a teammate. That's how teams play in sync. It takes a while to master, but when your team gets in that groove that is where champions are made and championships are won. There is nothing better than a team coming together to work as one and seeing the results.[112]

In my senior year, the chemistry and camaraderie on the team flowed into and impacted our private and personal lives. I made new friends and just had a great time. As a person of faith, it is important for me to share my faith, and because of all the relationships I built I was able to influence the lives of many. That year, I changed my school for God, and mentored a lot of people while playing ball.

COACHED FOR SUCCESS

As important as individual skills and team chemistry are, they cannot replace great coaching. And I believe I had some of the best. My freshman year, Coach Bean laid the foundation for my love of basketball. He inspired me to push hard and gave me opportunities to prove myself. In my sophomore year, I had Coach Harry Breland who took us all the way to South State Championship. He also coached me through my junior year, and he helped me develop confidence as a player. It was under Coach Breland that I became a starter. He also helped me begin

---

Lesson 112: Develop Team Chemistry. It is more fun playing the game with a group than being alone. Always take opportunities to play on a team. Life is about teamwork. It is all about who comes into your life and what you do with the knowledge they can pass on.

to appreciate the social aspect of the game. In my senior year, we had Coach Folkes. I had heard about him through a friend who had been coached by him for several years. She always bragged on him and how he would push you to be the best. So I looked forward to playing for him.

I learned a lot from Coach Folkes. I liked him because he was strategic and on top of his game. He wanted to win, and we felt that energy, but he also stayed approachable. It is great to have a coach that I could really talk to. We never felt he was bothered by us coming up to him. He showed us that he cared by listening and paying attention to our concerns. I think that made a difference in our devotion to him. Our win-loss record was pretty good that year. It ended up being a really great year for me.

Those days with Coach Folkes taught me to persevere even when I did not feel like it. He taught me to believe in myself, to walk tall and not to put myself down. I could be pretty hard on myself when I messed up a play, but I learned not to always zone in on the failures in a game. It was important to take a broader view, to see the bigger picture of how I contributed to the team. He always reminded us that it was a team effort. He motivated us to give 100 percent every time we went out on the court. To this day, his words encourage me to wake up every morning, work hard and end the day feeling and knowing that I did my best.[113] That is worth it all.

Having great coaching that last year of high school was so important. I ended the season with a strong support system that has carried me further in my career. Over the years as I have reflected on that last season of basketball and how strategic Coach Folkes' impact on me was, I am convinced that God placed him there for me. My only regret is that we did not win

Lesson 113: Put Value On Great Coaching. To be successful in the game of life, as in sports, you must be coached. I had great coaches that helped me throughout my career. Make sure you surround yourself with great coaches; people who will help you navigate life's greatest obstacles.

a championship that year, but knowing him, he would tell me to look at the bigger picture. I have kept in touch throughout the years, and I heard he took three teams of Lady Warriors basketball players to play in the South State Championships. He did an amazing job. He was a great coach on and off the court, and he deserves all the success in life.

ANOTHER MOUNTAIN TO CLIMB

Life does not cease once the game is won or lost. After you win or lose, there is always another game, another battle in another arena. Its outcome is determined by your mindset, your attitude and the way you choose to play the game.[114] Its winners have not been declared yet, and you are in the running for it. If you lost the previous game, you still have a chance to win the next one. Every single day, with the rising of the sun, life offers us another chance to be a winner. Sometimes it is a do-over but other times it is a completely new endeavor.[115]

Lesson 114: There's A Bigger Game With Greater Stakes. Be smart on and off the court. Always look at the big picture, beyond the game, beyond the court, beyond your teammates and into life itself. In other words, operate with your future in mind. The game of life is all about giving and taking. Always give back to others. Find your place and where you fit in. One way to do this is to try to help others get to where they are going. Amazingly, as you do this, you will also find your place.

Lesson 115: Never Give Up! If you are going for a new job or a position on a sports team and you don't make it, never give up. There was a time that I thought I was going to sell insurance. I took the exam four times and failed miserably all four times. That didn't hold me back. I just went a different route.

I tell many people that if they didn't get the job they interviewed for or weren't accepted into the college or degree program they wanted, they should not give up. Keep trying again and again. Even though I failed many times, I never gave up. I knew one day I would find success, and I did! My key to success was to never give up—and it's yours too!

Whatever form it takes, it's an opportunity to be a Champion and you must be ready for it.

If there is anything basketball taught me, it's the importance of a champions' mindset whether on or off the court, in practice or in a real game. I have learned that you must pay the price if you want to win, and you simply cannot win without a team. Keep preparing, and always see yourself as a Champion.[116]

FOREVER A CHAMPION

In my junior and senior years, my team did not win any championships, but it did not matter. The seeds of a champion had already been sown. I was a champion, and I graduated feeling like one. With the skills I had developed, I was ready to take my place beside my dad as our family continued to push for success, this time juggling college, work and the dream for better things. Several years later, I would fall in love, marry and have children, and juggle even more responsibilities as I pursued my dreams. But there is one thing that has not changed; I am Chantell, a Champion.

Lesson 116: Believe In A Better Future. *The champion believes in a better tomorrow, and keeps believing in spite of what the scoreboard says. That is what keeps him motivated through the downtimes. During a game, there is a certain amount of time set aside to play. Many times your team would have won; you just ran out of time. Never quit before the time runs out. Wins and losses are all opportunities to learn and to look ahead. It's hard to lose, but that is the game of life. You win some, and you lose some. Just remember to get back up and play again. The next time could be your big win.*

GAME OF LIFE
DISCUSSION FORUM

To join other winners in discussing the lessons from this book, join the Game of Life forum on Chantell's website.

www.ChantellMayesCooley.com

COMING SOON!

In the "GAME OF LIFE" Series

From
Chantell M. Cooley

If you love to journal, **The Game Of Life Journal** is for you. Based on the lessons in Chantell's book **Winning The Game of Life**, the journal is filled with inspiring quotes to help you start and end your day motivated and encouraged. As well, it has practical lessons that will equip you with wisdom to navigate some of the critical issues you face daily at home and in the work place.

The purpose of **Equipped For The Game of Life** is to provide a strategic and systematic approach to mentoring. Inspired by and based on the book **Winning The Game of Life** by Chantell Cooley, the book seeks to provide a whole-person approach to preparing people for the challenges of life whether they are found at home, in college or in the workplace. It equips them with tools that are not part of the traditional college curricula, but are vital for the growth and development of the young adult.

APPLY FOR SCHOLARSHIPS

From
Chantell M. Cooley

The Chantell Cooley Military Spouse Scholarship will cover up to $16,500 in one online degree program (associate, bachelor or master) at either Columbia Southern University or Waldorf University. The scholarship will be applied directly to the recipient's tuition for up to 60 semester hours or 24 consecutive months in the selected online degree program, whichever comes first.

For more information on criteria and how to apply visit Chantell's website.

www.ChantellMayesCooley.com

CHANTELL COOLEY LEADERSHIP
SCHOLARSHIP
FOR WOMEN

The Chantell Cooley Leadership Scholarship for Women provides financial assistance to young women seeking a residential degree at Waldorf University. These full tuition scholarships are awarded to women based on their leadership potential.

For more information on criteria and how to apply visit Chantell's website.

www.ChantellMayesCooley.com

3/11